Creating Your Own Space

Innovation and Activism in American Women's Writing

Series Editors: Sharon J. Kirsch, Arizona State University
and Janet Boyd, Fairleigh Dickinson Universit

This series focuses on writing by women who have sought to critique and transform their communities, countries, cultures, identities, or aesthetics. We invite monographs and edited collections of essays from established and emerging scholars that examine how women's writing questions, resists, subverts, or revises traditional gender roles, ways of knowing, ways of meaning/interpreting, and/or expectations of genre. This series features scholarship that expands theories, methodologies, and practices of established traditions or contributes to emerging innovative practices through the exploration of the inevitable connections between aesthetic forms and political, social, cultural, and/or historical contexts. Projects that pay attention to language and form, production and reception, practices of individual authors and collectives, and hybrid aesthetics are particularly welcome.

Recent Titles

Creating Your Own Space

The Metaphor of the House in Feminist Literature

María Davis

LEXINGTON BOOKS
Lanham • Boulder • New York • London

Published by Lexington Books
An imprint of The Rowman & Littlefield Publishing Group, Inc.
4501 Forbes Boulevard, Suite 200, Lanham, Maryland 20706
www.rowman.com

6 Tinworth Street, London SE11 5AL, United Kingdom

British Library Cataloguing in Publication Information Available

Library of Congress Cataloging-in-Publication Data Available

ISBN 978-1-7936-1535-0 (cloth)
ISBN 978-1-7936-1537-4 (pbk)
ISBN 978-1-7936-1536-7 (epub)

Contents

Acknowledgments

I would like to express sincere gratitude to the wonderful team of Lexington Books.

Thank you to my husband Jeremiah and my children Javier and Alexia for always being there for me.

Introduction

The relationship between women and houses has always been complex. Many influential writers have used the space of the house to portray women's conflicts with the society of their time. On the one hand, houses can represent a place of physical, psychological, and moral restrictions, and on the other, they often can serve as a metaphor for economic freedom and social acceptance. This usage is particularly pronounced in works written in the nineteenth and twentieth centuries, when restrictions on women's roles were changing: "anxieties about space sometimes seem to dominate the literature of both nineteenth-century women and their twentieth-century descendants."[1] This book uses a feminist literary criticism approach to examine the use of the house as metaphor in nineteenth- and twentieth-century literature. It also examines the dichotomy present in this metaphor in feminist literature across various countries and genres in order to portray the ways in which patriarchy was sometimes resisted and defied in the books of the time.

In order to better understand the reasons for the use of the house as a metaphor by different writers, the author researched the historical context of novels and plays and explains how the context relates to the house as a metaphor. Each chapter consists of an analysis of two literary works and a particular metaphor, such as the house as a prison or the house as a place of economic freedom. Although many other works employ the same metaphors, the two works selected are clear representations of the topic at hand. Although well known, the works presented have not been studied through this perspective before in a consistent manner; the study of the space of the house in feminist literature is crucial to fully understanding these literary works.

In *The House on Mango Street* by Sandra Cisneros, the main character wishes to escape poverty and discrimination by owning a space of her own where she can write when she pleases. She expresses this in her novel when she mentions that she wants "Not a flat. Not an apartment in the back. Not a man's house. Not a daddy's. A house all my own."[2] In *A Room of One's Own*, an essay that argues for a literary and figurative space for female writers, Virginia Woolf uses the metaphor of the house to advocate for female autonomy and for a place to create a female literary tradition:

> One has only to go into any room in any street for the whole of that extremely complex force of femininity to fly in one's face. How should it be otherwise? For women have sat indoors all these millions of years, so that by this time the very walls are permeated by their creative force.[3]

Virginia Woolf's words indicate not only a need for a female literary tradition, but also demonstrate how society has incarcerated women in their homes forcing them to fulfill very limited roles:

> Literary women, like Dickinson, Bronte, and Rossetti were imprisoned in their homes, their father's houses; indeed, almost all nineteenth-century women were in some sense imprisoned in men's houses. . . . It is not surprising, then, that spatial imagery of enclosure and escape, elaborated with what frequently becomes obsessive intensity, characterizes much of their writing.[4]

This idea of female reclusion is also depicted by Charlotte Perkins Gilman in "The Yellow Wallpaper," which tells the story of a woman who is imprisoned by her husband in a room. She becomes obsessed with its wallpaper, which she believes has entrapped many women including herself, as can be observed in her comments to her husband and sister in-law: "I've got out at last," said I, "in spite of you and Jane. And I've pulled off most of the paper, so you can't put me back!"[5] This mad woman in the attic idea emerges from being a female in the nineteenth century, when religious beliefs led to the polarization of woman's image. She had only two choices; she could be like the Virgin Mary or like Eve, the traitor, the killer of men:

> Idealized, woman is the Virgin Mary, the nineteenth-century angel of the house, keeper of morality, the unsullied, desexualized innocent of the law courts. If she topples off her pedestal, she is transformed into a monster; a killer of men, a less than human creature with a fishy talk. The tension such cultural polarities can set up in the individual is great.[6]

In *Wide Sargasso Sea by* Jean Rhys, the main character also represents the crazy woman in the attic: she is locked up by her husband who accuses her of insanity once he has her money and loses interest in her. This sense of entrapment is emphasized in the novel through the description of her environment and the attic room where she is imprisoned. The main character cannot see outside because the window is locked and "you cannot see out of"[7] it and "the door of the tapestry room is kept locked."[8] According to

Sandra M. Gilbert and Susan Gubar, Gothic ancestral mansions like the ones described in "The Yellow Wallpaper" and *Wide Sargasso Sea*, "explore the tension between parlor and attic, the psychic split between the lady who submits to male dicta and the lunatic who rebels."[9] In both stories, the main characters find a way to rebel against the imposed patriarchal norms, whether creating a double, like in "The Yellow Wallpaper" or setting the house on fire, like in *Wide Sargasso Sea*.

This anxiety about space is not only characteristic of the female Gothic, but also expands to other genres:

> In the genre Ellen Moers has recently called "female Gothic," for instance, heroines who characteristically inhabit mysteriously intricate or uncomfortably stifling houses are often seen as captured, fettered, trapped, even buried alive. But other kinds of works by women—novels of manners, domestic tales, lyric poems—also show the same concern with spatial constrictions. [10]

In *The House of Mirth*, a novel of manners, Edith Wharton uses the house as a metaphor for women's search for a new place in New York's changing society at the end of the nineteenth century. As society changed due to the effect of industrialization, urbanization, and the rise of the middle class, a redefinition of roles occurred that propagated certain stereotypes as a way for men to regain control over women: "It certainly is no coincidence that the moment the 'new women' started to demand their independence, the glorification of the housewife, of the angel in the house, took hold of society with unprecedented vigour."[11] In order to limit women to certain roles, respectability was emphasized, and those who were not considered respectable were shunned by society. If that was the case, the only options for women were going to the workhouse or being prostitutes, which in Victorian society was a term not just for street whores, but also one used for unmarried mothers, unfaithful wives, mistresses, artists and actresses. The main character of *The House of Mirth* is ostracized by her society because of a rumored relationship with a married man, and as a result, she dies alone in a poor house. She was never taught a profession, but instead how to be charming in order to find a husband and become a beautiful ornament in his house. Wharton was a decorator and a house designer and often referred to her own life as a house with secret rooms, an "inner house":

> I have sometimes thought of a woman's nature being like a house full of rooms: there is the hall through which everyone passes in and out and the drawing room where one receives formal visits . . . but beyond that, far beyond, there are other rooms, the handles of whose doors are never turned, no one knows the way to them, no one knows whither they lead; and in the innermost room, the holiest of holies, the soul sits and waits for a footstep that never comes. [12]

Like Wharton, other women have often described themselves as a house and Erik Erikson used the theory of the "inner space" to account for little girls' interest in houses. However, Sandra M. Gilbert and Susan Gubar believe that this description of women as houses only delegates them to the position of an object to be owned:

> To become literally a house, after all, is to be denied the hope that spiritual transcendence of the body which, as Simone de Beauvoir has argued, is what makes humanity distinctively human. Thus to be confined in childbirth (and significantly "confinement" was the key nineteenth-century term for what we would now, just as significantly, call "delivery") is in a way just as problematical as to be confined in a house or prison. [13]

During the last half of the nineteenth century, houses become domestic theaters, where a woman's sense of identity often came from her ability to perform the role of an entertainer. The main character in *The Awakening* by Kate Chopin belonged to the upper class, where she had to conform to the world's expectations of her, being a devoted mother, a beautiful wife, and an entertainer to her husband and his friends in his house. If she did not follow the rules, she had to pay for it. Neither Lily in *The House of Mirth* nor Edna in *The Awakening* followed the rules of social performance and were so unhappy that they committed suicide: as women they had no economic power without a man, and saw no way out of their situation.

The literary connection between women and houses, and the view of the house as a place of imprisonment is also reflected in drama. Henrik Ibsen and Federico Garcia Lorca, among many others playwrights, use the house as a central metaphor for women's experience. In their plays, the house meant a place of moral, physical, and emotional confinement. Ibsen's *A Doll House* is one of the clearest examples in drama of the complex relationship between women and houses in the nineteenth century. In this case, the main character refuses to continue with a life in which women had only two possible roles in society, being obedient housewives and dedicated mothers, so she slams the door of her house in her husband's face in order to discover who she really is:

Helmer: You are first and foremost a wife and a mother.

Nora: I no longer believe that. I believe that I am first and foremost a human being, just as much as you—or at least, that I will try to become one. [14]

In *The House of Bernarda Alba*, Lorca depicts women's situation in Spain in the twentieth century, where they were physically and psychologically imprisoned in their houses due to the restrictive roles their society imposed on them, one of them being the obsolete tradition that women could not leave their house for years after one of their parents died. In the second act of the play, Adela, one of the female characters, complains about the freedom that men have versus women and expresses how she wishes she could leave the house just to enjoy nature outside, and says: "*¡Ay, quien pudiera salir también a los campos!*" ["Man, how I wish I could too go outside to the countryside!"].[15]

For minority populations living in the United States, the house is also an important metaphor, often one of social integration and economic success. In works like *Brown Girl, Brownstones* by Paule Marshall and *A Raisin in the Sun* by Lorraine Hansberry, we can observe Black American families' struggle to succeed in the United States, which is represented by the ownership of a home. In Marshall's novel, the mother of the main character works several jobs in order to purchase a Brownstone, the dream of all the Barbadian Americans who come to this country: "The West Indians, especially the Barbadians who had never owned anything perhaps but a few poor acres in a poor land, loved the houses with the same fierce idolatry as they had the land on their obscure islands."[16]

A Raisin in the Sun tells the story of an African American family whose mother inherits money and decides to purchase a home in a white neighborhood because it is cheaper. However, the racist white neighbors do not want them there and send the realtor to buy the house back from them. This story focuses on the importance of owning a house as a symbol of social and economic success for Black Americans. The strong female characters in these works represent the strength that Black Americans must possess to achieve their dream of owning a house.

The topic of the importance of the house in feminist literature is also present in Latin America in the 1980s, when we start to see female boom writers such as Isabel Allende and Laura Esquivel embrace the significance of houses. In *The House of the Spirits* by Allende and *Like Water for Chocolate by* Esquivel, the authors use magic realism to portray how women defy the patriarchal tradition of restricting women to the space of the house. With magic realism as their literary device, both authors show how women rebel against the roles that society tries to impose on them. In Allende's case, her character Clara resists the interpretation of the house as a place of male political control by transforming it into her own magic world:

> In response to Clara's imagination and the requirements of the moment, the noble, seigniorial architecture began sprouting all sorts of extra little rooms, staircase, turrets, and terraces. Each time a new guest arrived; the bricklayers would arrive and build another addition to the house. The big house on the corner soon came to resemble a labyrinth.[17]

In Esquivel's case, her main character Tita escapes the obsolete patriarchal tradition that forbids the youngest daughter from marriage because she has to take care of her parents. Tita is able to break free by transforming the kitchen into a magical place in which she controls everyone's lives by influencing their behavior through her culinary rituals: "The kitchen becomes a mystical abode in which the protagonist is empowered and permitted to re-create reality in order to avoid social and spiritual annihilation."[18] Both Clara and Tita are able to escape their confinement at home by creating their own magical worlds.

The following chapters will explore each of these themes in more detail, demonstrating the central role that houses play in feminist literature.

NOTES

1. Sandra M. Gilbert and Susan Gubar, *The Madwoman in the Attic: The Woman Writer and the Nineteenth-Century Literary Imagination* (New Haven and London: Yale University Press, 2020; 1984), 83.

2. Sandra Cisneros, *The House on Mango Street* (Vintage Books, 2009), 108.

3. Virginia Woolf, *A Room of One's Own* (Mariner, 1989), 88.

4. Sandra M. Gilbert and Susan Gubar, *The Madwoman in the Attic: The Woman Writer and the Nineteenth-Century Literary Imagination*, ed. cit., 83.

5. Charlotte Perkins Gilman, "The Yellow Wallpaper" (Sweden: Wisehouse Classics, 2016), 30.

6. Sandra M. Gilbert and Susan Gubar, *The Madwoman in the Attic: The Woman Writer and the Nineteenth-Century Literary Imagination*, ed. cit., xiii.

7. Jean Rhys, *Wide Sargasso Sea* (London & New York: Norton, 2016), 161.

8. Ibidem, 163.

9. Sandra M. Gilbert and Susan Gubar, *The Madwoman in the Attic: The Woman Writer and the Nineteenth-Century Literary Imagination*, ed. cit., 86.

10. Ibidem, 83.

11. Sarah Kuhl, "*The Angel in the House* and Fallen Women: Assigning Women their Places in Victorian Society," open.conted.ox.ac.uk, *Open Educational Resources* (July 11, 2016): 172. https://open.conted.ox.ac.uk/resources/documents/angel-house-and-fallen-women-assigning-women-their-places-victorian-society.

12. From Dennis Krausnick's play *The Inner House*, an adaptation of Wharton's autobiography called *A Backward Glance*, 1934.

13. Sandra M. Gilbert and Susan Gubar, *The Madwoman in the Attic: The Woman Writer and the Nineteenth-Century Literary Imagination*, ed. cit., 89.

14. Henrik Ibsen, *A Doll's House* (New York: Global Classics, 2014), 64.

15. Translated by me. Federico Garcia Lorca, *Three Plays: Blood Wedding, Yerma, The House of Bernarda Alba*, Trans. Michael Dewell and Carmen Zapata, Farrar (New York: Straus and Giroux, 1993), 883.

16. Paule Marshall, *Brown Girl, Brownstones* (New York: Dover Publications, 2009; 1959), 8.

17. Isabel Allende, *The House of the Spirits* (New York: Atria, 2015), 299.

18. Rosa Fernández-Levin, "Ritual and Sacred Space" in Laura Esquivel's *Like Water for Chocolate, Confluencia*, Vol. 12, No. 1 (Fall 1996), University of Northern Colorado: 106.

Chapter One

The House as a Symbol of Women's Economic Freedom

The House on Mango Street *and* A Room of One's Own

Both Sandra Cisneros and Virginia Woolf consider owning a house a symbol of independence and the only way to have the chance to be a successful writer. In the book *The House on Mango Street*, Cisneros depicts her personal experiences as a woman in a Mexican-American patriarchal society. She explores the experience of being caught between Mexican and Anglo-American cultures, facing the misogynist attitudes present in both of these cultures, and experiencing poverty. As a young girl in the 1960s, Cisneros dealt with challenges related to the formation of her Chicana identity. There were seven children in her family, and her family members did not initially support her writing, especially her father who never wanted her to be an author. *The House on Mango Street* is also about the subject of migration, as she had to move from house to house because of her family's economic struggles. Cisneros created Esperanza, the main character of the book, because she wanted to portray how she felt displaced as a young woman trying to be a writer. As a person of color and as a woman with a low socioeconomic status, Cisneros felt discriminated against while studying at the University of Iowa and therefore, in *The House on Mango Street*, she depicts her longing to have a space of her own through her main character Esperanza. To Cisneros, having a space of her own meant having financial and sexual freedom and having a place to write. At the same time, Virginia *Woolf's A Room of One's Own* asserts that women need a place and economic resources to be successful writers and therefore redefine women's roles in society.

1

Although the two authors come from different countries, social classes, and races, they both stress the need for women's economic independence and the need for a space to express themselves as independent human beings despite the expectations for women in their societies. Woolf's narrator points out that women have not been given the same opportunities as men and have not had access to education or an intellectual legacy. Men have used their literature and history to affirm the inferiority of women and to protect their own superiority. That is why Woolf finds it essential for women to be able to have a space to write, so they can write their own stories and experiences in which they are empowered.

THE HOUSE ON MANGO STREET

The House on Mango Street is a collection of poems and short stories based on the author's life and the women living in her poor Latino neighborhood of Chicago. The voice in the book is the main character's Esperanza, who is largely based on Cisneros's life. Cisneros grew up in poverty with seven brothers and never had a beautiful house in which to live:

> We didn't always live on Mango Street. Before that we lived on Loomis on the third floor, and before that we lived on Keeler. Before Keeler, it was Paulina, and before that, I can't remember. But what I remember most is moving a lot. Each time it seemed there'd be one more of us. By the time we got to Mango Street, we were six—Mama, Papa, Carlos, Kiki, my sister Nenny and me. [1]

The author's longing for a house of her own is portrayed in her main character's search for a decent place to live. For Cisneros, having her own space represented escaping from male domination and poverty and being able to create your own success. In Esperanza's case, it was the same:

> Not a flat. Not an apartment in the back. Not a man's house. Not a daddy's. A house all my own. With my porch and my pillow, my pretty purple petunias. My books and my stories. My two shoes waiting beside the bed. Nobody to shake a stick at. Nobody's garbage to pick up after. [2]

In *A House of My Own: Stories from My Life*, Cisneros's longing for a house and her disappointment in the house that her parents bought is represented in Esperanza's inability to accept the house on Mango Street as her own. When talking to Alicia, one of the characters in the book, Esperanza tells her: "No, this isn't my house I say and shake my head as if shaking could undo the year I've lived here. You have a home, Alicia, and one day you'll go there, to a town you remember, but me I never had a house, not even a photograph . . . only one I dream of." [3] A house, to Cisneros, also meant a place where you could write as well. In *A House of My Own: Stories from My Life*, she compares owning a house with owning a writing machine: "A house. A writing machine. These two go hand in hand for me. A home makes me feel like writing. I feel like writing when I'm at home."[4]

For Esperanza, living in Mango Street meant not being able to write because of her lack of having a place to write, meaning her own proper space free of distractions. She was expected to perform other duties because she was a woman. This is also portrayed in the book in the case of Mamacita in the chapter "No Speak English" or the case of Sally in "What Sally Said." In the first case, Mamacita feels imprisoned in a poor ugly house that she cannot leave because she does not speak English. In Sally's case, it becomes a place of torture because of her father's physical abuse toward her. Living in Mango Street meant accepting the limiting roles imposed on women by society, in which the only options were being a mother and wife, or a sex object. All these roles are represented by the women who surround Esperanza: her mother, her neighbors, and friends. In the story "And Some More," for instance, two young girls talk about the nature of snow and say: "There ain't thirty different kinds of snow, Lucy said. There are two kinds. The clean kind and the dirty kind, clean, and dirty. Only two. There are a million zillion kinds, says Nenny. No two exactly alike. Only how do you remember which one is which?"[5] Initially, the girls' conversation appears to be just childish nonsense. However, Nenny and Lucy's words highlight a conflict that is at the heart of Cisneros's work, which is portraying the only two roles possible for women in her society: a virgin or a prostitute. Cisneros highlights the difficulties inherent in this dichotomy because it does not allow women to be their own unique individuals. Cisneros is not the only writer to acknowledge the challenges in dealing with this duality, as Luis Leal observes, "the characterization of women throughout Mexican literature has been profoundly influenced by two archetypes present in the Mexican psyche: that of the woman who has kept her virginity and that of the one who has lost it."[6] These archetypes, which we can observe in stories about la Malinche, the violated woman, and la Virgen de Guadalupe, the Holy Mother, reflect female roles in Mexican culture based on their sexuality and influence people's perceptions of femininity in the Latin American world. The character that most reflects this duality in *The House on Mango Street* is Esperanza's friend, Sally. On different occasions in the book, Sally is identified either as la Malinche or la Virgen de Guadalupe. Her life reveals both the objectification and confinement associated with each archetype. In the chapter called "Sally," her physical description connects her with sexuality. She has "eyes like Egypt and nylons the color of smoke," and her hair is "shiny black like raven feathers."[7] Because her looks are perceived as a sign of promiscuity, she is stigmatized at school, the boys tell stories about her, and she has very few female friends. Her father confines Sally to her room because he says "to be this beautiful is trouble."[8] Like la Malinche, Sally's sexuality is a threat to her father's masculinity. In fact, her father physically abuses her by beating her until her "pretty face [is] beaten and black" because "[h]e thinks [she's] going to run away like her sisters who made the family ashamed."[9] Sally's father uses violence to contain her threatening sexuality. Similar to Sally in *The House on Mango Street*, all the female characters are trapped in an abusive relationship, poverty, or teenage motherhood. Nevertheless, Cisneros uses her main character, Esperanza, as an example of hope, as her name indicates in Spanish. She is portrayed as a strong character who finds a way to fight patriarchal oppression and racism. In the chapter called "Those Who Don't," Esperanza discusses how other ethnicities, mainly white, feel scared when they run into dark-skinned people like her. In the chapter titled "Red Clowns," Esperanza is assaulted and referred to as "Spanish girl," which is stereotypically associated with loose sexuality. When she is being cat-called, they refer to her as a "little Spanish girl." The theme of sexual harassment and sexual abuse is present throughout the novel, and it is depicted as one of the many ways men attempt to control and dominate women. An example of this is that Sally, mentioned above, escapes from her father's violence only to be abused by her husband, who beats her.

Another obstacle to freedom that the women on Mango Street have to overcome is poverty. As noted above, Esperanza comes from a low-class Chicano family that has to move from place to place and ends up in a bad neighborhood on the outskirts of Chicago. In the chapter called "Bums in the Attic," Cisneros reminds us of how Esperanza's family, much like her own, would go to an affluent neighborhood on Sundays to fantasize about one day owning a beautiful house like the ones in that neighborhood. In Esperanza's words: "I want a house on a hill like the ones with the gardens where Papa works."[10] Cisneros insists on the idea that the American dream is present in every culture within the United States, and it is reinforced unto the proletariat. This is not the only Marxist theory instilled in this novel. In the chapter called "Our Good Day," Esperanza expresses the excitement of her friends and her own, gained by purchasing a bicycle together to share: "The bike is three ways ours, says Rachel who is thinking ahead already. Mine today, Lucy's tomorrow and yours day after."[11] The happiness created by economic freedom, even if the object has to be shared among others, creates a sense of hope, as it is also portrayed in the chapter called "Alicia Who Sees Mice." In this chapter, a little girl is forced to take the role of a grown woman because her mom is dead. Still, she refuses to give up her dream of going to a university and obtaining a higher paying job: "Alicia, who inherited her mama's rolling pin and sleepiness, is young and smart and studies for the first time at the university. Two trains and a bus, because she doesn't want to spend her whole life in a factory or behind a rolling pin."[12] Both this character and Esperanza represent how economic freedom is the way to a better future for Chicanas. So again, we see that economic and sexual freedom in

The House on Mango Street is represented by owning a nice house. This house also represents a place to grow as a writer. In *A House of My Own: Stories of My Life*, Cisneros admits that Gaston Bachelard's *The Poetics of Space* has a considerable influence on her writing because he believes that "the house shelter's day-dreaming, the house protects the dreamer, the house allows one to dream in peace."[13] Cisneros mentions that in the search for her last house, she is looking for a place "to protect [her] from folks who want to interrupt [her] writing . . . a fortress for the creative self."[14]

A ROOM OF ONE'S OWN

In *A Room of One's Own*, Virginia Woolf explains how women were kept from doing the things that they wanted, among them writing, because of the roles they were forced to play in society and their lack of economic freedom. Woolf believes that women need "money and a room of their own"[15] in order to fulfill their dreams.

Both in the "Introductory Letter" and *A Room* the notion of "the room" serves as a potent political metaphor for women's needs because it concretizes visually, tactilely the politicization of the personal and the political. The achieving of personal space in *A Room*, as opposed to simple place within someone else's framework, makes woman into a respected citizen, constitutes her as a political subject.[16] Woolf uses the metaphor of the room to describe not only women's political needs but also to explain how women must step out of the roles that society has imposed on them, which are limited to being a mother and a housewife, if they want to be free. In her opinion, women need economic freedom, represented by the metaphor of a "room," or a house, to be able to do whatever they please. Women writers must have a room of their own and time away from husbands and children to be able to write and leave an accurate vision of what women are like, which can only happen if the books about women are written by women. Woolf notes this will create a literary tradition that will encourage other women to write as well.

In *A Room of One's Own*, an essay based on two lectures that Woolf was asked to give in an all-female college on Women and Fiction, she tells the story of a fictional character called Mary Beton, who sits on the lawn of a college campus, Oxbridge, and is ordered off the grass and forbidden access to the library because she is female. The next day, she visits the British Museum Library, where she notices that all the scholarship on women has been written by angry men. When she turns to history books, she realizes that little has been written about women's daily lives, which makes her create her own fictional character, Shakespeare's sister, who does not succeed as a writer because she is a woman, even though she is as talented as her brother. The next day, Mary sees a man and a woman go in a taxi together, which gives her the idea that maybe everyone has a male and a female inside that have to be united to create a great book: "It is when this fusion takes place that the mind is fully fertilized and uses all its faculties."[17] Woolf finishes her lecture by telling women that they need five hundred pounds a year and a room of their own to be able to produce a genius piece of writing.

Among other things, Wolfe's work was meant to address the contemporary notion that women produced inferior literary work compared to men. In *A Room of One's Own*, Woolf reminds the women in the lecture hall, and her wider audience, how women were denied the time and space to do any creative work because they also had to do household chores and take care of their children and their husbands. She explains how "It would have been impossible completely and entirely, for any woman to have written the plays of Shakespeare in the age of Shakespeare,"[18] not because of lack of skills, but because of lack of time, a space of their own, economic resources, and society's expectations of women. As a young woman, Woolf had to fight her own father to educate herself in a community that thought that only men should be taught. Through her work, she demonstrated that given the same conditions, women could be as good at writing or anything else as men.

The fact that women have to continually fight for the freedom to choose a career and prove their worth against society's expectations of them causes them to struggle with their own identity sometimes. Woolf's main character, Mary Beton, struggles with her own place in the world and her own identity. In chapter 1, Woolf says: "Call me Mary Beton, Mary Seton, Mary Carmichael or any other name you please—it is not a matter of importance."[19] This comment also indicates that Woolf's narrator could be any woman, which universalizes the reader's experience. She adds that women's roles in literature have been idealized while real women were being mistreated at home:

> Women have burnt like beacons in all the works of all the poets from the beginning of time—Clytemnestra, Antigone, Cleopatra, Lady Macbeth, Phèdre, Cressida, Rosalind, Desdemona, the Duchess of Malfi, among the dramatists; then among the prose writers: Millamant, Clarissa, Becky Sharp, Anna Karenina, Emma Bovary, Madame de Guermantes—the names flock to mind, nor do they recall women "lacking in personality and character." Indeed, if a woman had no existence save in the fiction written by men, one would imagine her a person of the utmost importance; very various; heroic and mean; splendid and sordid; infinitely beautiful and hideous in the extreme; as great as a man, some think even greater. But this is a woman in fiction. In fact . . . she was locked up, beaten and flung about the room.[20]

Woolf continues to say:

> A very queer, composite being thus emerges. Imaginatively she is of the highest importance; practically, she is completely insignificant. She pervades poetry from cover to cover; she is all but absent from history. She dominates the lives of kings

and conquerors in fiction; in fact, she was the slave of any boy whose parents forced a ring upon her finger. Some of the most inspired words, some of the most profound thoughts in literature, fall from her lips; in real life, she could hardly read, could scarcely spell, and was the property of her husband.[21]

Woolf questions the roles that society imposes on women by examining history itself, showing the disparity between the image of women in fiction and women in real life. In *A Room of One's Own*, Woolf makes her reader reevaluate the truth in history books by explaining the subjectivity of truth. She forces the reader to rethink the accepted opinions on reality, so they question their view on history, which was mainly written by men. In the second chapter, she explained how "One must strain off what was personal and accidental in all those impressions and so reach the pure fluid, the essential oil in truth."[22] Woolf fictionalizes *A Room of One's Own*, demonstrating this synthesis of fact and fiction. She also examines her historical period and questions the context in which women are judged. Woolf gave presentations at several women's colleges and reminded them of these principles, also explaining to them how, even though they had the privilege of an education, they were still limited in the roles they could fulfill in their society: "Now it is my belief that this poet who never wrote a word and was buried at the crossroads still lives. She lives in you and me, and in many other women who are not here tonight, for they are washing up the dishes and putting the children to bed."[23] She encouraged them to fight against the expectations that were meant to keep women under men's subjugation. Woolf believes that the reason that women are treated unequally by men in literature, history, and in life, in general, is because men need to reinforce their own confidence as the more capable sex. She thinks that despite this fact, women continue fighting to be the best they can be: "It calls for gigantic courage and strength. More than anything, perhaps, creatures of illusion that we are, it calls for confidence in oneself."[24] The fight for equality and a woman's literary tradition that Woolf mentions begins with economic freedom, represented by having a space of your own. As she explains in her conclusion to her lecture *A Room of One's Own*, "it is far more important to know how much money women had and how many rooms than to theorize about their capacities."[25] According to Solomon, "The room even visually concretizes the aspirations of Woolf's new political woman of 1929, a woman, who like 'Shakespeare's sister' longs to follow in the footsteps of her brother."[26]

Although Woolf and Cisneros come from different countries, races, economic backgrounds, and time, they both left us with a robust literary legacy on how to empower women in society. They agree that education and financial independence are the key to women's freedom so they can create their own destiny and fight whatever roles society may try to impose on them. They believe that if women have economic independence, they will be able to make their own voices heard and continue with the tradition of empowering other women through literature. The search for a house in Cisneros's *The House on Mango Street* and the search for a room in Woolf's *A Room of One's Own* is none other than the search for a voice, a woman's voice. Cisneros and Woolf found their voices through creating a space of their own and would like to ensure that other women do so as well.

NOTES

1. Sandra Cisneros, *The House on Mango Street*, ed.cit., 3.
2. Ibidem, 108.
3. Ibidem, 106.
4. Sandra Cisneros, *A House of My Own: Stories from My Life* (Vintage Books, 2001), 6.
5. Sandra Cisneros, *The House on Mango Street*, ed. cit., 35.
6. Leslie Petty, "The Dual-ing Images of la Malinche and la Virgen de Guadalupe in Cisneros's *The House on Mango Street*" (Critical Essay), *MELUS*, Vol. 25, No. 2 (Summer 2000).
7. Sandra Cisneros, *The House on Mango Street*, ed. cit., 81.
8. Ibidem.
9. Ibidem, 92.
10. Ibidem, 86.
11. Ibidem, 15.
12. Ibidem, 31–32.
13. Sandra Cisneros, *A House of My Own: Stories from My Life*, ed. cit., 348.
14. Ibidem, 349.
15. Virginia Woolf, *A Room of One's Own* (Mariner, 1989), 3.
16. Julie Robin Solomon, "Staking Ground: The Politics of Space in Virginia Woolf's *A Room of One's Own* and *Three Guineas*," *Women Studies*, Vol. 16 (1989): 331–332.
17. Ibidem, 98.
18. Ibidem, 5.
19. Ibidem.
20. Ibidem, 43.
21. Ibidem, 43–44.
22. Ibidem, 25.
23. Virginia Woolf, *A Room of One's Own*, ed. cit., 57.
24. Ibidem, 112.
25. Ibidem, 105.
26. Julie Robin Solomon, "Staking Ground: The Politics of Space in Virginia Woolf's *A Room of One's Own* and *Three Guineas*," ed. cit., 335.

Chapter Two

The House and Female Mental Entrapment

"The Yellow Wallpaper" and Wide Sargasso Sea

In "The Yellow Wallpaper" by Charlotte Perkins Gilman and *Wide Sargasso Sea* by Jean Rhys, two stories in the genre of female Gothic narrative, the house represents the institution of marriage and works as a symbol of female entrapment by patriarchal society. "In this genre, where the subversive nature of the text appears uppermost, in its dark and prison-like images of feminine experience within domesticity, marriage threatens to become the ultimate prison."[1] In both novels, the female characters are deprived of their freedom and accused of insanity by their husbands because the wives were of no use to them anymore, a situation only made possible due to women's lack of economic means once they were married.

"THE YELLOW WALLPAPER"

"The Yellow Wallpaper" was published in 1892 in *The New England Magazine*. It is written in first person by a woman whose husband, a physician, diagnoses her with a "temporary nervous depression," and then secludes her in the attic of an old mansion. Because she is depressed, has nothing to do, and is forbidden to work or write, she becomes obsessed with the yellow wallpaper in her room and imagines a woman behind the wallpaper pattern who wants to get free. Throughout the novel, she tells her husband on many occasions that she does not feel well, but he ignores her calls for help, isolates her from the outside world, and fails to give her the medication she needs, so she ends up losing her mind.

Gilman believed that domestic architecture was responsible for the weak-ening of the human race, specifically women: "Her utopian designs for kitch-enless houses, communal nurseries, and public canteens were intended to draw women through to the public side of the wall where, she believed, dwelt civilization."[2] In female Gothic literature, the house portrays the dichotomy in women's desires for protection and the entrapment that the institution of marriage meant for them. Other experts in female Gothic literature agree that the house in Gothic fiction is "the place from which some (usually fallen men) are locked out, and others (usually innocent women) are locked in."[3] In female Gothic fiction, the house is a place of entrapment where the dark side of motherhood and marriage can be observed. In this context, "the heroine's active exploration of the Gothic house in which she is trapped is also an exploration of her relation to the maternal body that she shares, with all its connotations of power over vulnerability to forces within and without."[4] Because she has no autonomy and cannot control her destiny, the narrator's identity is threatened. The Freudian concept of the double is reflected in "The Yellow Wallpaper" when the main character sees this threat to her identity. She sees herself reflected as a woman trapped behind the yellow wallpaper trying to escape:

> As soon as it was moonlight and that poor thing began to crawl and shake the pattern, I got up and ran to help her.
> I pulled and she shook, I shook and she pulled, and before morning we had peeled off yards of that paper.[5]

The concept of the double is obvious when she says: "I can see her out of every one of my windows!"[6] She not only sees herself in the woman behind the yellow wallpaper, but also in her reflection in the windows. Because she is locked up in a room with nothing to do, she is projecting another self outside of that room. A free self.

When Gilman's main character refers to the pattern on the yellow wallpa-per, it addresses the oppressive structure of patriarchy. She is trying to rip apart the unfair rules that have kept women hostage for generations: "They get through, and then the pattern strangles them off and turns them upside down, and makes their eyes white!"[7] In fact, the image of the eyes appears several times throughout the book. At the very beginning of the story, the narrator explains referring to the yellow wallpaper's pattern: "I get positively angry with the impertinence of it and the everlastingness. Up and down and sideways they crawl, and those absurd, unblinking eyes are everywhere."[8] These unblinking eyes refer to all the women whose freedom has been sup-pressed by the patriarchal society in which they lived. However, they are escaping the pattern of the yellow wallpaper, a male dominated world, one by one: "Sometimes I think there are great many women behind, and sometimes only one, and she crawls around fast, and her crawling shakes it all over."[9] Women in the Victorian era, like the narrator, had no autonomy because they had no money or properties of their own. Once they were married, everything they owned belonged to their husbands, including themselves, which is why they are trying to escape that reality.

The married woman of the period was frequently commodified and became *a femme couverte* under established law—a woman whose autonomy and identity were denied as she was regarded as her husband's property. Under such circumstances, marriage signaled a figurative death for women.[10] The main character's attempt to find her identity and establish her autonomy is clear when she secretly writes her version of the story, in which she says that her husband "hates to have [her] write a word"[11] and ignores the fact that she is truly suffering: "John does not know how much I really suffer. He knows there is no reason to suffer, and that satisfies him."[12] Even though she is suffering from postpartum depression, her husband only diminishes her feelings and tells her to have "will and self-control and not let any silly fancies run away with her."[13] This behavior is associated with the idea prevalent in patriarchal societies that men are rational creatures, while women are irrational and hypersensitive. Her husband's pressure for her to ignore her feelings and emotions, along with her confinement to the attic, causes her to become obsessed with her house, with the yellow wallpaper in her room specifically, representing her oppressive marriage. This sense of entrapment is reflected in the analogy established between her room and a room in an asylum for the mentally ill. Her bed is nailed to the floor, the windows are barred, and there is a gate at the head of the stairs, all of which adds to the reality of imprisonment. Her room could also be associated with a torture chamber: "To date, critics have overlooked the torture chamber associations of this paraphernalia of confinement."[14] The fact that her husband was a doctor and was believed to have the knowledge to diagnose her condition made no one believe her, so she was forced to find a mental way out by freeing the woman in the wallpaper.

Women are depicted as crazy when they do not want to conform to the patriarchal norm and the narrator indicates this through the fact that the main character destroys all the yellow wallpaper. This destruction could be interpreted as her destroying a male tradition that depicts women in a negative way. The imposition of the patriarchal values could have killed her sanity, but she has freed the rest of the women from being defined by men. By writing her own story in secret, the narrator has continued with the female literary tradition that show that the reasons for women's insanity are the roles imposed on them by a patriarchal society. Gilman felt abandoned and mistreated by men, finding it difficult to publish her work as a female in a male dominated literary world. She therefore writes a story of a woman who, despite being held prisoner in her own house, is able to write her story and figuratively escape her prison by creating a double, the woman in the yellow wallpaper: "I've got out at last," said I, "in spite of you and Jane. And I've pulled off most of the paper, so you can't put me back!" Now why should that man have fainted? But he did, and right across my path by the wall, so that I had to creep over him every time![15]

The main character has ripped all the wallpaper, all the rules that were imposed on her by society, so she will escape her prison, even if she has to figuratively "creep over" her husband every time.

WIDE SARGASSO SEA

Another important book in the female Gothic genre is *Wide Sargasso Sea*, which tells the story of Bertha, one of the characters from *Jane Eyre* by Charlotte Bronte. Antoinette, later referred to as Bertha by her husband, is the daughter of white slave owners in Jamaica in the nineteenth century. She lives in a run-down estate called Coulibri with her mother, Annette, and her sickly brother Pierre. They became poor in 1833 when her father died five years earlier and the slaves where freed, leading to the ruin of many slave owners. They lived among freed slaves who hated them until her mother, who used to own slaves, decides to marry an English man, Mr. Mason, to escape poverty. One night, the freed slaves accidentally set her mother's house on fire, injuring her bother Pierre, who finally dies. Her mother never forgives her husband for not leaving Coulibri earlier despite the fact that she constantly asked him to do so, and then loses her mind because of Pierre's death. Antoinette is injured in the fire and is at first cared for by her Aunt Cora, but she is later sent to a convent for several years. When she is seventeen, Antoinette's stepbrother marries her off to an English gentleman, Mr. Rochester, who only marries her for her money. Antoinette and Mr. Rochester then move back to Jamaica, a place that he finds as strange and mysterious as his new wife. Although he is sexually attracted to her initially, the situation changes when he receives a letter by a supposedly mixed race brother of Antoinette, in which the brother writes that Antoinette is crazy, like her mother. Antoinette tries desperately to regain her husband's attention and asks one of her servants, Christophine, to give her a potion to make her husband pay attention to her again, but it does not work. Christophine advises her to leave him, but he has control of her money now and she does not think he would give her any to survive. He has sexual relations with one of the servants next door to her bedroom, leading her into a deep depression, which he considers madness. Shortly thereafter, they move to England where he decides to lock her up in the attic under the supervision of a servant. Antoinette completely loses notion of time and reality, attacking her stepbrother with a knife when he visits her, and dreaming several times that she escapes the room and sets the house on fire. One night, she wakes up from that dream and feels she must act on it. The novel ends with Antoinette holding a candle and walking downstairs.

Like "The Yellow Wallpaper," *Wide Sargasso Sea* is based on the idea that the main character's madness is caused by the patriarchal society rules of nineteenth century England and the institution of marriage, which leads to the main character being locked up in an attic. Once married, women had no possibility to have money of their own and their husbands owned their property leaving no way out of a bad marriage, and therefore no way out of their own house. This sense of entrapment appears from the beginning of the story and persists throughout. The fires at the beginning and end of the book are connected. In both fires, an encaged bird dies because his wings are clipped, and he cannot fly away. Dandicat, in the introduction to the edition of this novel, explains how "Coco's death symbolized a whole lot more than the passing of a single animal, but Coco had been so carefully and powerfully drawn that he became one of many characters I mourned."[16] Coco's death in the fire symbolizes women's situation in nineteenth-century England. They were trapped in a house, with no economic power and therefore at the mercy of their husbands, who call them crazy and locked them up, if it was convenient to them.

This entrapment is evident when Antoinette is being forced to marry Mr. Rochester and he explains that she made "an effort to escape";[17] however, he convinced her to not leave by telling her he would protect her. In an analysis of the book, Lydon suggests that "Antoinette finds patriarchal abodes to be confining or dangerous in some way."[18] Mr. Rochester not only does not protect her, but physically abuses her, as indicated in the words of Christophine, one of her servants: "I see you very rough with her eh?"[19] Ellis asserts that "Thus the middle-class idealization of the home, though it theoretically protected a woman in it from arbitrary male control, gave her little real protection against male anger."[20] Because of this abuse, it is necessary for the main character to escape from her home: "As in *Jane Eyre*, patriarchal homes in *Wide Sargasso Sea* are so dangerous that it is necessary for the female protagonist to leave home."[21] Christophine implores Antoinette: "Pack up and go";[22] however, Antoinette has no money of her own, which prevents her from escaping her husband. That is why Christophine tells her that she has "no husband, I thank my God. I keep my money. I don't give it to a worthless man."[23] To which Antoinette says: I have no money of my own at all, everything I had belongs to him. . . . That is English law."[24] According to Lydon, it is "Antoinette's failure to leave a patriarchal home [that] leads to madness and imprisonment in *Wide Sargasso Sea*, and as Rhys suggests, to her demise in *Jane Eyre*."[25]

Because Antoinette cannot leave Mr. Rochester, he continues to abuse her both physically and psychologically. When he loses complete interest in her

sexually, he starts calling her by a different name, Bertha, in order to deprive
her from her original identity:

> Don't laugh like that, Bertha
> My name is not Bertha; why do you call me Bertha?
> Because it is a name I'm particularly fond of. I think of you as Bertha.[26]

Antoinette tells Mr. Rochester not to call her Bertha, but he ignores her. By
doing this, he transforms her into someone that she is not: "Bertha is not my
name. You are trying to make me into someone else, calling me by another
name."[27] His sleeping with another woman is one more example of how he
continues to torture her, because he engages in this behavior in the room next
to his wife's so she can hear it. This situation makes her very upset and she
stops taking care of herself. In Mr. Rochester's words: "The door of Antoinette's room opened. When I saw her I was too shocked to speak. Her hair
hung uncombed and dull into her eyes which were inflamed and staring, her
face was very flushed and looked swollen. Her feet were bare."[28] Her husband's infidelity causes her to start drinking and drives her into a deep
depression. She becomes a zombie. He says that she becomes "Like a doll.
Even when she threatened me with the bottle she had a marionette quality."[29]
When Christophine confronts Mr. Rochester, she tells him that one of the
reasons Antoinette is not well is because he starts calling her names. "Marionette. Some word so,"[30] which causes her to have an identity crisis. When
Christophine asks him to give her half of her money back so she can fall in
love again and be happy, he reacts with anger: "A pang of rage and jealousy
shot through me then."[31] And then he continues to says "I'll take her in my
arms, my lunatic. She's mad, but *mine, mine*."[32] In other words, even though
he does not love her, he still considers her his property and would rather lock
her up in an attic than allow her to be happy with anyone else. In Christophine's words: "You want her money but you don't want her. It is in your
mind to pretend she is mad. I know it. The doctors say what you tell them to
say."[33] And that is exactly what he does, he takes her out of her town in
Jamaica and brings her to England to lock her up in his attic: "She's one of
them. I too can wait—for the day when she is only a memory to be avoided,
locked away, and like all memories, a legend. Or a lie."[34] With this reference
to a memory or a lie, he means that he hopes that she will be forgotten, that
no one will remember that she ever existed or what happened to her. He
wants to delete her from existence and his way of accomplishing this goal is
by imprisoning her in his attic.

   In fact, the house where Mr. Rochester locks up Antoinette is described
like a prison, as we can observe in the emphasis on the thickness of the walls:
"The thick walls, she thought. Past the long gate a long avenue of trees and
inside the house the blazing fires and the crimson and white rooms. But

above all the thick walls, keeping away all the things that you have fought till you can fight no more."[35] The idea of imprisonment and isolation she feels persists when she tells us that "The door of the tapestry room is kept locked."[36] Antoinette is so disconnected from the rest of the world that she loses her sense of time and begins to think that she is in a "cardboard world" instead of in England: "This cardboard house where I walk at night is not England."[37] Another example of her disconnection is that she believes she sees her mother look away from her in a tapestry hanging on the wall next to her room: "Looking at the tapestry one day I recognized my mother dressed in an evening gown but with bare feet. She looked away from me, over my head just as she used to do. I wouldn't tell Grace this."[38] The tapestry itself is a symbol of female entrapment, like the yellow wallpaper, in which the narrator sees women hiding behind the pattern, trying to escape. Antoinette's mother might be trying to escape the tapestry like her daughter is trying to escape from the attic in which she is locked up.

Both Rhys, the author of *Wide Sargasso Sea*, and Antoinette are unable to find a safe place because the traditional patriarchal home is a place of "danger and imprisonment."[39] Since Rhys does not think that she belongs, the way to find her home is by writing these stories. She feels like she does not belong anywhere, like her main character in *Wide Sargasso Sea*: "So between you I, I often wonder who I am and where is my country and where do I belong and why was I ever born at all."[40] Antoinette, like Rhys, is caught in limbo because of her geographic and racial background. England was described in the novel as cold and distant and Jamaica was like a feverish dream where her servants called her "white cockroach."[41] These two geographical locations could not be more different, and Rhys, like Antoinette, did not feel that she belonged in either of those places: "Rhys resided within the unfixed space between Dominica and England. She felt exiled; as if she belonged to no nation."[42] By giving voice to the woman in the attic, Rhys not only shows how the reasons for her so called insanity were the patriarchal society she lived in and the institution of marriage in particular, but she also creates a textual home for herself and a literary tradition for other women to follow. According to Trihn H. Minh-ha, "the true home is to be found, not in houses, but in writing."[43] Philp agrees with this idea, according to him, "Rhys seeks 'a room of one's own' in the actual practice of writing, and through the textualization of place she allows herself to search for 'home.'"[44] As it is mentioned in Erica L. Johnson's *Home, Maison, Casa*, "At a certain moment for the person who has lost everything, whether that means a being or a country, language becomes the country."[45] Rhys did not only find a home through her writing, but she also gave a voice to the unheard women in the nineteenth century. The main character in *Wide Sargasso Sea*, might have been locked up in an attic for years, but she finds a way out and burns the house that was entrapping her: "Now at last I know why I was brought here and what I have to do. There must have been a draught for the flame flickered and I thought it was out. But I shielded it with my hand and it burned up again to light me along the dark passage."[46]

Both "The Yellow Wallpaper" and *Wide Sargasso Sea* tell the stories of women who were locked up in their houses and considered insane because they did not conform to the rules their societies imposed on them. Their lack of economic freedom prevented them from taking action and saving themselves from the neglect and aversion of their husbands. However, as can be seen in both "The Yellow Wallpaper" and *Wide Sargasso Sea*, there is still light "along the dark passage."[47] There is still hope that women will fight to have control of their own lives through economic freedom.

NOTES

1. Carol Margaret Davidson, "Haunted House/Haunted Heroine: Female Gothic Closets in 'The Yellow Wallpaper,'" *Women Studies*, Vol. 33, No. 1 (2004): 55.

2. Kathy Farguharson, "The Last Walls Dissolve: Space Versus Architecture in *The Memoirs of a Survivor* and 'The Yellow Wallpaper,'" *Doris Lessing Studies*, Vol. 28, No. 1 (2009): 4.

3. Kate Ellis, "Can you Forgive Her? The Gothic Heroine and Her Critics," *A Companion to the Gothic*, ed. David Punter (Oxford: Blackwell, 2000), ix.

4. Claire Kahane, "The Gothic Mirror," *The Mother Tongue: Essays in Feminist Psychoanalytic Interpretation*, eds. Shirley Nelson Garner, Claire Kahane and Madelon Sprengnether (Ithaca and London: Cornell UP, 1985), 338

5. Charlotte Perkins Gilman, "The Yellow Wallpaper" (Sweden: Wisehouse Classics, 2016), 28.

6. Ibidem, 26.

7. Ibidem, 26.

8. Ibidem, 16.

9. Ibidem, 26.

10. Carol Margaret Davidson, "Haunted House/Haunted Heroine: Female Gothic Closets in 'The Yellow Wallpaper,'" ed. cit., 55.

11. Charlotte Perkins Gilman, "The Yellow Wallpaper," ed. cit., 14.

12. Ibidem.

13. Ibidem.

14. Carol Margaret Davidson, "Haunted House/Haunted Heroine: Female Gothic Closets in 'The Yellow Wallpaper,'" ed. cit., 59.

15. Ibidem, 30–31.

16. Jean Rhys, *Wide Sargasso Sea* (London and New York: Norton, 2016), 8.

17. Ibidem, 82.

18. Susan Lydon, "Abandoning and Re-inhabiting Domestic Space in Jane Eyre, Villette and Wide Sargasso Sea," *Bronte Studies*, 35, 1, 26.

19. Jean Rhys, *Wide Sargasso Sea*, ed. cit., 139.

20. Kate Ferguson Ellis, *The Contested Castle: Gothic Novels and the Subversion of Domestic Ideology* (University of Illinois Press, 1989), xi.

21. Susan Lydon, "Abandoning and Re-inhabiting Domestic Space in Jane Eyre, Villette and Wide Sargasso Sea," ed. cit., 27.

22. Jean Rhys, *Wide Sargasso Sea*, ed. cit., 99.

23. Ibidem, 11.

24. Ibidem.

25. Susan Lydon, "Abandoning and Re-inhabiting Domestic Space in Jane Eyre, Villette and Wide Sargasso Sea," ed. cit., 27.

26. Jean Rhys, *Wide Sargasso Sea*, ed. cit., 122.

27. Ibidem, 133.

28. Ibidem, 132.

29. Ibidem, 136.

30. Ibidem, 139.

31. Ibidem, 144.

32. Ibidem, 150.

33. Ibidem, 145.

34. Ibidem, 156.

35. Ibidem, 160.

36. Ibidem, 163.

37. Ibidem.

38. Ibidem, 162.

39. Kate Ferguson Ellis, *The Contested Castle: Gothic Novels and the Subversion of Domestic Ideology*, ed. cit., x.

40. Jean Rhys, *Wide Sargasso Sea*, ed. cit., 93.

41. Ibidem, 20.

42. Alexandra Philp, "The Geography of Jean Rhys: The Impact of National Identity upon the Exiled Female Author," *Transnational Literature*, Vol. 9, No. 1 (November 2016): 3.

43. Trinh H. Minh-ha, "Wanderers Across Language," *Elsewhere, Within Here: Immigration, Refugees and the Boundary Event* (London: Routledge, 2011), 34.

44. Alexandra Philp, "The Geography of Jean Rhys: The Impact of National Identity upon the Exiled Female Author," ed. cit., 8.

45. Erica L. Johnson, *Home, Maison, Casa: The Politics of Location in Works by Jean Rhys, Marguerite Duras, and Erminia Dell'Oro* (London: Fairleigh Dickinson University Press, 2003), 13.

46. Jean Rhys, *Wide Sargasso Sea*, ed. cit., 171.

47. Ibidem, 171.

Chapter Three

The House as a Metaphor for Social Performance

The House of Mirth *and* The Awakening

Although women's status was slowly improving at the beginning of the twentieth century as they received permission to attend universities and occupy certain job positions, women's financial dependence on men and the expectations for women to follow societal rules still persisted. Women were still considered men's possessions and their house was a place where they were expected to entertain their husbands and his guests. One way in which men tried to impress others was by having a beautiful wife and a beautiful home. The house became a social place where women had to perform their role of mothers, wives, and entertainers: "the home became a stage setting for the gala social events orchestrated and acted out by women. The upper-class home functioned less as a private haven from the competition of the marketplace than as the public stage for that competition."[1]

Both Lily Bart, the main character in *The House of Mirth*, and Edna, the main character in *The Awakening*, came from the upper class, where a woman's sense of identity often came from her ability to perform the role of entertainers for others in their society. In order to belong, they had to conform to what their world expected of them; if they did not, they had to pay for it: "Emblematic of woman's role in the new urban culture—more visible, more powerful, and yet more alienated, more commodified, more of an aesthetic object—the leisure-class woman's privilege and power comes at a great price."[2] During the last half of the nineteenth century, houses became domestic theaters. In fact, a new preoccupation with interior design emerged during this time. Wharton herself wrote a book called *Decoration of Houses* in 1897 in which she discussed how she would like to reconfigure public and private spaces: "it is only necessary to observe the planning of the average house to see how little this need is recognized,"[3] a reference to the importance of the house as a place for entertainment. During the early 1900s, the house started to express the personality of its occupants. In other words, women's self-worth began to be related to their ability to have a beautiful house where they had to be charming and entertain men. Codman asserts that: "What makes Lily's character so compelling is the extent to which she embodies the psychic and cultural shifts of her time, a time when the self as a moral character was giving way to the self as a personality to be "performed."[4]

If women did not fulfill the roles expected of them during the nineteenth, early twentieth century, and even today, they were criticized and ostracized. Neither Edna nor Lily follow the social performance rules and were therefore unhappy. In fact, we will soon see that they committed suicide because as women, they had no economic power without a man. They had no possibility of survival unless they were married and conformed with what their society expected of them, which was entertaining their husbands and his friends, and being good mothers, leaving them no choice but death.

THE HOUSE OF MIRTH

Edith Wharton's novel tells the story of Lily Bart, a girl in her late twenties during the first part of the twentieth century in New York. Lily is powerless as a woman and completely dependent on getting married in order to survive in her society because, even though she was originally from an affluent family, they are ruined by an unspecified financial reversal. Lily is later orphaned and then minimally supported by her aunt, Mrs. Peniston. She is admitted by the New York high society because of her beauty and lineage, but she does not have the economic means to support herself or to maintain her friends' lifestyle. She goes into debt by gambling and commits the mistake of asking one of her friend's husbands, Gus Trenor, for help. To recover what she lost, she asks him to invest some of her money in the stock market on her behalf, but he deceives her by telling her that she is more than $10,000 in debt. Rumors start to circulate that she is behaving inappropriately with Mr. Trenor, and she is then ostracized by society, causing her prospects of marriage to disappear. After her aunt disinherits her, she has to work for a living for the first time in her life. Within a few weeks, she loses her job as an apprentice in a millinery shop because she is not able to do her job well, which makes her realize that: "She had been fashioned to adorn and delight; to what other end does nature round the rose leaf and paint the humming-bird's breast? And was it her fault that the purely decorative mission is less easily and harmoniously fulfilled among social beings that in the world of nature?"[5] Wharton's intention with her novel is clear: "In a patriarchal society, women serve as a merely 'ornamental' function; they are passive, physically attractive commodities rather than active, purposeful agents."[6] At the end of the novel, Lily tells her friend Lawrence Selden: "I am a very useless person. I can hardly be said to have an independent existence. I was just a screw or a cog in the great machine called life, and when I dropped out of it I found I was of no use anywhere else. What can one do when one finds that one only fits into one hole? One must get back to it or be thrown out into the rubbish heap- and you don't know what it's like in the rubbish heap!"[7]

Lily's descent from riches to rags and her resulting suicide is caused by her lack of a stable home in a society that requires women to be home entertainers:

> After her father's death, Lily is literally homeless, as she and her mother "wandered from place to place, now paying long visits to relations whose house-keeping Mrs. Bart criticized, and who deplored the fact that she let Lily breakfast in bed when the girl had no prospects before her, and now vegetating in cheap continental refuges, where Mrs. Bart held herself fiercely aloof from the frugal tea-tables of her companions in misfortune."[8]

The House of Mirth's plot consists of Lily moving from one house to another because of her economic inability to have her own home without a husband: "The power of the novel comes not from Lily's function as a mere symptom of historical and economic pressures, but from the complex narrative and affective processes by which she negotiates homes and their loss or collapse."[9] Lily goes from Selden's flat at the beginning of the novel, to Gus Trenor's mansion, then to Aunt Peniston's mansion, later on to Nettie Struther's flat, and finally, to her boarding house: "Lily's experience of movement between homes leads to nostalgia—which in turn serves as a management device to soften the reality of her constant displacement."[10] Lily is in between spaces and cannot fulfill her role as a home ornament and entertainer unless she finds a husband that can provide her with a house to live in. Her time is running out and so are her options to marry someone in her high society since she does not follow her friends' advice to make herself available to the right wealthy gentleman.

In Wharton's fiction, the house is not only a place to live and entertain in; it is also a representation of the self: "Wharton erects houses as definitive representations of the self and its place in society; that is, Wharton produces a concept of the self through metaphors of drastically interiorized structures and perfect enclosures."[11] In *The House of Mirth*, the self is equivalent to its social relations. In other words, you are nothing unless you are invited to certain events with specific people: "In *The House of Mirth*, a woman's clothing, her social position, her public behavior, the manner in which she carries herself, all appear to anchor society, to formulate social class, and in turn, to bring individual consciousness into being."[12] When defining individual self worth, decoration, art and fabric are very important, as can be seen by the many events that take place in people's houses in *The House of Mirth*. Lily's internal deterioration is represented by the deterioration of the spaces, the many houses she inhabits or frequents throughout the course of the novel. She goes from being invited to mansions and luxurious flats to dying alone in a boarding house. In Wharton's novels, "the space is not rejuvenating or healing, but rather, brings a solitude commensurate with loneliness, pain and even death."[13] Wharton insists that what she calls "the real self" in the context of the novel only exists if it is related to the social self, which could not exist without a physical place: "In the Wharton text houses signify a heightened cultural consciousness in that they announce social status, establish families, exclude marginal individuals; in addition, houses become models for the architecture of the mind."[14] Lily has to perform a specific role in these different houses in order to have the chance of finding a husband and having a house of her own and economic stability. She "is extremely invested in herself as an object. Her own best stage manager, Lily is the creator, director, and producer of some of the most striking scenes in the novel."[15] McGee agrees that: "Throughout most of the novel, dinners are the stage for an obligatory performance, a stage upon which one maneuvers for position, makes connections, watches others for potential weaknesses, and, with luck, is oneself seen to advantage."[16]

The first house Lily visits is Selden's apartment, where she feels very comfortable and admits to the fact that although his female cousin, Gertrude Farish, who had an apartment of her own, was not looked upon well by her society and not marriageable, at least she was free: "She is free and I am not. If I were, I daresay I could manage to be happy even in her flat. It must be pure bliss to arrange the furniture just as one likes, and give all the horrors to the ash-man."[17] In this scene, Lily explains that she would like to have that freedom as well. Men have the choice to marry or not, like her friend Selden, but women are forced to enter into a marriage because they would not have a place to live otherwise: "There is a difference—a girl must, a man may if he chooses."[18]

In Bellomont, Lily feels divided: sometimes she acts like herself and openly flirts with Selden and other times, in front of her suitor Percy Gryce, she acts like an innocent woman in order to gain his approval and obtain a marriage proposal. This behavior shows the fine line along which women had to operate in order to be accepted by their society. They could flirt and look attractive but, at the same time, they had to look innocent enough to be marriage material. Lily had to perform this very delicate balance when she was in Bellomont, which is described as "a theater, a spectacle: it is a home where tradition is disregarded and the boundaries between public and private space give way."[19]

Going to church is also a social performance in *The House of Mirth*, as it can be observed in the Trenors' use of their omnibus to display their luxurious life:

> The observance of Sunday at Bellomont was chiefly marked by the punctual appearance of the smart omnibus destined to convey the household to the little church at the gates. Whether any one got into the omnibus or not was a matter of secondary importance, since by standing there it not only bore witness to the orthodox intentions of the family, but made Mrs. Trenor feel, when she finally heard it drive away, that she had somehow vicariously made use of it.[20]

Lily initially tries to use the church omnibus to her advantage in order to impress Gryce; however, she cannot imagine the boredom of a life with him and does not show up for their date, because "this is a performance she cannot seem to manage."[21]

The Wellington Bry's mansion is even more "well designed for the display of a festal assemblage."[22] This mansion and the people in it are described like an impressionistic painting, blending together to portray the exuberance and luxury of the upper class during the early twentieth century in New York. The characters are described as actors in a play and Lily as another performer. The mansion is a space where yet again she has to display herself as an ornament in order to find a husband: "Lily is a figure whose boundaries occasionally dissolve into the ornamental world that surrounds her. . . . She thrives in the luxuriant hot-house atmosphere of New York's mansions and begins to die only when she is driven out of them. Their furnishings are her soil, their mirrors are the pools in which she finds the security of her own reflected beauty."[23] In other words, Lily uses these elegant mansions as stages to perform the roles that she is expected to fulfill in her society.

Mrs. Peniston's home is viewed as the typical Victorian home where women's virtue should be protected and it is described as a fortress. When Lily lives in that environment with Mrs. Peniston, the house does not give her any sense of warmth or protection; on the contrary, it feels oppressive to her. "The house in its state of unnatural immaculateness and order was as dreary as a tomb."[24] Lily admits that "She had always hated her room at Mrs. Peniston, its ugliness, its impersonality, the fact that nothing in it was really hers."[25] She wants to find a place where she can "assert her own eager individuality."[26]

> When Lily takes a job as a secretary for Norma Hatch, she begins living in a room in the Emporium Hotel. In this section of the novel, Wharton em-

phasizes society's search for individual material pleasure and how it affects
women. Lily repeats the word "real" when she describes the environment of
the Emporium hotel and the new rich to criticize the consumer society of
the time that dictates not only how interior spaces should look, but also
what women should wear or buy. [27]

Women in this materialistic society are strongly influenced by trends, can
have no substance, and feel empty inside like Lily: "There is a homeless-
ness here of profound proportions, for not only are these women without a
domestic interior of their own, . . . they are without any traditions, any ties
to the past." [28] The superficiality forced upon women in a capitalist world
makes them feel empty, with Lily saying that her role as a woman in her
society leaves her feeling a "vast gilded void." [29]

The countryside plays an important role in the novel as well, as it is
considered an extension of the house for the upper class: "Nature acts as a
'living room' for Lily Bart's personality and self expression." [30] However,
much like the city mansions, these rural spaces, although idyllic in nature,
show the reduction of women's roles to entertainers and ornaments. Once
again, women had to aim to be part of the beautiful background by dress-
ing and acting in a certain way. Lily's internalization of her role as an
ornament can be observed in her disappointment while walking in the
gardens of Bellomont: she feels pretty but there is no one there to see her:
"the combination of a handsome girl and a romantic scene too good to be
wasted." [31] Lily was disappointed that she had no one watch her performance, the sole purpose of which was to find a rich husband to support
her because she had no chance of surviving on her own.

Due to Lily's refusal to marry someone only for money and because of
her dubious reputation after Mr. Trenor's deceit, she ends up working in a
factory and living in boarding houses in poor neighborhoods. One day,
she runs into Nettie Struther, a lower-class woman who she had helped in
the past, and she brings Lily to her modest home. Her meeting with Nettie
makes Lily reflect on her own life and the meaning of a home. Nettie is
not an ornament or entertainer for anyone; she works and shares her life
difficulties with her husband George: "In Wharton's version of the senti-
mental home, propriety does not come before love, and the fallen woman
is not punished. Men and women work together. . . . Wharton imagines
not woman being confined in the home, but a more egalitarian compan-
ionate marriage within that home." [32] In this part of the book, Wharton
emphasizes how homes should not be a place where women are just ornaments or the embodiment of someone's wealth, but a place where women
should share the household responsibilities with men and be respected and
loved for who they are.

THE AWAKENING

Kate Chopin wrote this novel, originally titled *A Solitary Soul*, in 1899. *The Awakening* tells the story of Edna Pontellier, a 28-year-old woman who lives on Grand Isle, Louisiana. She is married to Leonce, who works during the week and leaves her to take care of their two children. Edna spends most of her time with her friend Adele Ratignolle, the typical "mother-woman" who only exists to take care of her children and husband. One day, Edna befriends Robert Lebrun, an attractive man from the island, and falls in love with him. For her, being with Robert represents freedom, which is the opposite of being the "mother-woman" that her society expects her to be. As time passes, Edna becomes more independent, recalls her past relationships, wishes she were young again, begins painting, and develops a sense of self that is apart from her domestic roles. When Edna's friend Mademoiselle Reisz plays the piano for her, she starts to enjoy music as part of her new self. She also learns how to swim, which gives her a sense of independence and freedom. By the end of the summer, she has grown apart from her husband Leonce and is still in love with Robert, who leaves for Mexico to prevent them from committing adultery. She is devastated by his departure, although he promises to write to her. Edna and Leonce return to New Orleans, where Edna continues to paint and to see her friend Mademoiselle Reisz, who reads Robert's letters to her and encourages her to pursue him. Meanwhile, her husband consults with Dr. Mandelet, a family friend, on his wife's new behavior. Dr. Mandelet suspects that Edna is cheating on her husband but does not tell him and advises Robert to let her be. Leonce leaves for a business trip and his mother agrees to care for the kids so that Edna has a break. Edna realizes how much she enjoys being alone and moves to a smaller house and becomes more economically independent by selling her paintings. She has a romance with the town womanizer Alcee Arobin; she does not actually care for Alcee but uses him as a substitute for Robert's affection. When Robert comes back from Mexico, Edna invites him to her new place and kisses him. However, he tells her that he cannot be with her because she is married and belongs to another man, even though she tells him that she does not belong to anyone. In that moment, they find out that Mademoiselle Reisz is sick, and Edna has to go help her. He promises to come back the next day, but never does. When she comes back to the house, she finds a note that he left her that says: "I love you. Good-by—because I love you." Edna spends the night thinking of her children and her relationships. The next day, she goes to Grand Isle, determined not to let anyone control her, not even her children, and commits suicide by drowning herself.

When Chopin's novel was first published, it had a very negative reception because her portrayal of female marital infidelity shocked the nineteenth-century critics. The novel was later forgotten, and it was not until the 1969 with the publication of two volumes, *Kate Chopin: A Critical Biography* and *The Complete Works of Kate Chopin*, that the novel became part of the literary canon. *The Awakening* follows the trend of *The Scarlet Letter*, *Madame Bovary*, *Anna Karenina* and *Effie Briest* in their concern for nineteenth-century women and their treatment as objects in marriage and motherhood. During the time that *The Awakening* was published, the idea of "True Womanhood," which required self-sacrifice, was changing in favor of freedom and personal fulfillment, due in large part to an expansion of women's rights in the United States. Women began to have more economic and legal independence and began to see the advent of the "New Woman," a woman with more freedom. Nevertheless, the portrayal of women in literature by male writers, such as Charles Dickens or Mark Twain, which idealized the concept of "Angel in the House" made this new freedom more difficult to achieve for women as it continued to depict the only possible roles for women in society as mother and wife. Chopin was very concerned with the "mother-woman" role, which we can see represented in the character of Adele. Adele symbolized the values of "True Womanhood," a Victorian principle on women's sexual and maternal performances: "The novel's representation of the self-abnegation demanded by the Victorian social and religious institution of motherhood is communicated via a thinly veiled tone of derision."[33] Edna explains at the beginning of the novel that, like Adele, "there were women who idolized their children, worshipped their husbands, and esteemed it a holy privilege to efface themselves as individuals and grow wings as ministering angels."[34] Edna starts to realize that she does not want to be the "angel in the house" because she would like to have the freedom to choose the roles that she performs in society. When her husband returns from a trip, wakes her up, and requires her total attention, she tries to ignore him, but he pretends that one of her sons has a fever and accuses her of being a bad mother if she refuses to attend to him right away. She knows her son does not have a fever and that her husband is inventing this story to pay her back for not giving him attention; however, she feels completely controlled by her husband and pressured to be a mother: "An indescribable oppression, which seemed to generate in some unfamiliar part of her consciousness, filled her whole being with a vague anguish. It was like a shadow, like a mist passing across her soul's summer day. . . . She was just having a good cry all to herself."[35] As we can observe, Edna's husband does not consider her an equal, but a piece of property that he owns. When he sees that she had tanned too much at the beach, he becomes disappointed and tells her: "You are burnt beyond recognition."[36] Feminist critics agree that this sentence reveals "the dominant proprietorial ideology behind capitalist economics. Mr. Pontellier sees his wife as his wife, that is, something he owns, rather than an individual."[37]

In addition to being pressured to follow the wife and the "mother-woman" role, Edna feels isolated because she does not belong among her husband's Creole friends: "Mrs. Pontellier, though she had married a Creole, was not thoroughly at home in the society of Creoles; never before had she been thrown so intimately among them. There were only Creoles that summer at Lebrun's. They all knew each other, and felt like one large family,"[38] Edna was forced to perform the mother and wife role in front of her husband's friends even though she felt that she did not fit in that role and that she did not belong. Indeed, the only person that she enjoyed spending time with other than Mademoiselle Reisz was Robert. Nevertheless, the line between behavior that was viewed as being a pleasant hostess to your husband's friends and behavior that what was too flirtatious and inappropriate for a married woman was very fine. Edna had to learn to navigate her society's expectations of her of being pleasant to other men without being too forward. In the end, she could not help falling in love with Robert and she had to pay for it with her life, because women who stepped outside their marriage were considered prostitutes and were scrutinized and ostracized. Edna knew that, and had no choice but to commit suicide, because she had already committed social suicide by committing adultery.

In the Victoria era, the marital house represents the place where women have to perform society's expectations of them. Edna's decision to leave the house where she lived with her husband and kids and move to her own house at the end of the novel indicates her intention to step outside the roles of being a mother and a wife so she could find herself. Through the new economic freedom Edna achieved by selling her paintings, she is able to afford a space of her own. Nevertheless, the fact that Edna's new house is called "the pigeon house" serves as a premonition to the tragic ending. Even though Edna is initially happy in her new small house, she realizes that owning her own house is still does not allow her to be herself and achieve the true freedom that she wants. Many more changes had to happen for women in the nineteenth century for them to feel a sense of self-ownership in their society. The pigeon house can be seen as a birdcage, representing the societal rules that women cannot escape. Even with a house of her own, Edna is still considered her husband's possession, as we can observe in Robert's skepticism when she tells him that she no longer belongs to her husband and can do whatever she wants: "His face grew a little white. 'What do you mean?' he asked."[39] Robert sees her freedom from her husband as an impossibility, which leaves Edna no way out. Death by drowning is seen in the novel as the only freedom possible in a world that oppresses women and forces them to perform very restrictive roles at the cost of their happiness. As Edna submerges herself in the ocean "She felt like some new-born creature, opening its eyes in a familiar world that it had never known. . . . She thought of Leonce and the children. They were a part of her life. But they need not have thought that they could possess her, body and soul."[40] Peter Ramos believes that "Edna's sense of an ending suicide serves as a warning of what could happen to a protagonist who seeks unattainable freedom by rejecting all available social roles."[41] The depiction of Edna's tragic ending in *The Awakening* demonstrates that, in order to be happy, women needed to be able to choose more roles than the ones offered to them in their society.

Edna, unlike Lily, found a house of her own, but that was not enough for her to be happy. Women in the Victorian era were in a disadvantaged position by not being allowed to have economic and sexual freedom. Once again, we see that women had to depend on marriage for their happiness, and if their husbands could not provide them with it, they were doomed. Both Edna and Lily refused to perform the roles that society imposed on them of marrying for money and being men's ornaments and entertainers, so they chose death instead of an unfulfilled life:

> In Edith Wharton's *The House of Mirth*, Lily Bart's vacillation about marriage to a (or any) wealthy businessman represents her reluctance to accept a role for which she seems ill-suited. In Kate Chopin's *The Awakening*, Edna Pointellier discovers—during a summer on Grand Isle—that she is neither a "mother woman" nor a "networker": she is unwilling to sacrifice herself for her children or for the sake of receiving the wives of her husband's business associates. Both Lily Bart and Edna Pontellier choose to end their own lives rather than persevere in an unreceptive world.[42]

Both Lily and Edna decide to choose who they want to love instead of letting society dictate it, rejecting their roles as objects of exchange and entertainment imposed by social capitalism. In this context, upper class houses and mansions functioned as the stages where women were expected to engage in social networking, whether to find a husband or to entertain their husband and his friends or to raise their kids. In the late nineteenth and early twentieth century, houses transformed into public spaces where women were considered ornaments for their husbands' display; however, Lily and Edna decided to die instead of allowing others to treat them like objects.

NOTES

1. Amy Kaplan, *The Social Construction of Realism* (Chicago: University of Chicago Press, 1988), 93.

2. Thorstein Veblen, *The Theory of the Leisure Class* (New York: Penguin Books, 1967), 180.

3. Edith Wharton; Ogden Codman Jr., *The Decoration of Houses* (London: B.T. Batsford, 1898), 22.

4. Nancy Von Rosk, "Spectacular Homes and Pastoral Theaters: Gender, Urbanity and Domesticity in The House of Mirth," The John Hopkins University Press, *Studies in the Novel*, Vol. 33, No. 3 (Fall 2001): 331.

5. Edith Wharton, *The House of Mirth* (South Carolina: Columbia, 2020), 134.

6. Tom Quirk and Gary Scharnhorst, "Feminism," *American History Through Literature: 1870–1920*, Vol. 1 (Thomson and Gale, 2006): 385.

7. Edith Wharton, *The House of Mirth*, ed. cit., 139.

8. Diane E. McGee, *Writing the Meal : Dinner in the Fiction of Twentieth-Century Women Writers* (Toronto: University of Toronto Press, 2002), 43.

9. Sean Scanlan, "Going no Place?: Foreground Nostalgia and Psychological Spaces in Wharton's *The House of Mirth*" *Style*, Vol. 44, Nos. 1 and 2 (Spring/Summer, 2010): 207.

10. Ibidem, 215.

11. Jill M. Kress, *The Figure of Consciousness: William James, Henry James, and Edith Wharton* (New York and London: Routledge, 2002), 132.

12. Ibidem, 132–133.

13. Ibidem, 134.

14. Ibidem.

15. Ibidem, 139.

16. Diane E. McGee, *Writing the Meal: Dinner in the Fiction of Twentieth-Century Women Writers*, ed. cit., 44.

17. Ibidem, 5.

18. Ibidem, 7.

19. Nancy Von Rosk, *Spectacular Homes and Pastoral Theaters: Gender, Urbanity and Domesticity in The House of Mirth*, ed. cit., 335.

20. Edith Wharton, *The House of Mirth*, ed. cit., 32.

21. Ibidem.

22. Ibidem, 38.

23. Quoted in Nancy Von Rosk, *Spectacular Homes and Pastoral Theaters: Gender, Urbanity and Domesticity in The House of Mirth*, ed. cit., 338–339.

24. Edith Wharton, *The House of Mirth*, ed. cit., 58.

25. Ibidem, 9.

26. Ibidem, 67.

27. Nancy Von Rosk, *Spectacular Homes and Pastoral Theaters: Gender, Urbanity and Domesticity in The House of Mirth*, ed. cit., 340.

28. Ibidem, 341.

29. Edith Wharton, *The House of Mirth*, ed. cit., 123.

30. Nancy Von Rosk, *Spectacular Homes and Pastoral Theaters: Gender, Urbanity and Domesticity in The House of Mirth*, ed. cit., 341.

31. Edith Wharton, *The House of Mirth*, ed. cit., 35.

32. Nancy Von Rosk, *Spectacular homes and Pastoral Theaters: Gender, Urbanity and Domesticity in The House of Mirth*, ed. cit., 346.

33. Amanda Kane Rooks, "Reconceiving the Terrible Mother: Female Sexuality and Maternal Archetypes in Kate Chopin's *The Awakening*," *Women's Studies*, Vol. 45 (2016): 124.

34. Kate Chopin, *The Awakening*, 2015, 9.

35. Ibidem, 7.

36. Ibidem, 44.

37. J. Killeen "Mother and Child: Realism, Maternity, and Catholicism in Kate Chopin's *The Awakening*," *Religion & the Arts*, Vol. 7, No. 4 (2003): 413.

38. Kate Chopin, *The Awakening*, ed. cit., 9.

39. Ibidem, 89.

40. Ibidem, 95.

41. Peter Ramos, "Unbearable Realism: Freedom, Ethics and Identity in *The Awakening*," *College Literature*, Vol. 37, No. 4 (2010): 147.

42. J. Judge, "On Their Own: Women Taking Control of Their Lives," *Changing English: Studies in Reading & Culture*, Vol. 10, No. 2 (2003): 175–184.

Chapter Four

The House as a Symbol of Female Physical Entrapment

A Doll House *and* La casa de Bernarda Alba

Both Henrik Ibsen's *A Doll House* and Federico García Lorca's *The House of Bernarda Alba* depict the house as a place of moral entrapment where women are forced to occupy the roles that their patriarchal societies impose upon them.

The relationship between women and houses is clearly reflected in literary drama, particularly in the late nineteenth century. Many plays explore the complicated relationship between female characters and their houses, including *A Cherry Orchard*, *The Three Sisters*, *The Seagull* and *Uncle Vanya* by Chekov. Other significant examples of the relationship between women and their houses are in plays by Ibsen, such as *The Master Builder*, *Hedda Gabler*, and especially *A Doll's House*. In these plays, the connection between women and houses and the division between the public and the private space is clear, and it is often considered to stem from the implementation of the *skene* in ancient Greece, where males occupied the public space, the *polis*, and women the private one, the *oikos*. This tradition led to the retreat of women to the area of their houses, so they go unseen: "The face of the house thus marks the barrier between the genders, and it is only on the threshold that man and women can meet."[1] In *A Doll's House*, Nora, the main character, was confined to her house and could only occupy the role of a mother and a wife. Her life was reduced to being her husband's doll, his possession. She was not considered a human being, but her husband's entertainer. Nora's restrictive role might be explained by the fact that *A Doll's House* was written in Norway in 1879, a time in which women could only be concerned with raising their children and matters of entertainment, such as playing instruments, singing, and cooking. And in the United States, Thomas Jefferson indicated that: "Female education should concentrate on ornaments and the amusements of life . . . dancing, drawing, and music."[2] Women could not be fully educated or independent; they had to rely entirely on their husbands. At the end of *A Doll's House*, Nora slams the door of her house in her husband's face, leaving him and her children, to try to discover who she really is. She realizes that until that point in her life, she has only performed the roles that society wanted her to perform and that she has to leave the confinement of her house in order to find herself.

In *The House of Bernarda Alba*, Federico García Lorca exposes women's situations in Spain in the first half of the twentieth century by using the metaphor of the house as a moral prison. In this play, Bernarda, a mother of five girls, loses her second husband and forbids her daughters from leaving the house for eight years. This constraint goes against her daughters' desires, eventually causing her youngest daughter's death after she rebels against her mother and society's norms by sneaking away with her older sister's fiancé.

A DOLL'S HOUSE

This play portrays a couple, Nora and Helmer Torvald, who seem happy from an outsider's perspective. Helmer has a health issue and cannot work, so Nora asks one of Helmer's coworkers, Krogstad, for a loan so she can take her husband to Italy to recover from his illness. However, Nora does not want her husband to feel emasculated in the eyes of his male colleagues by helping him, so she tells him that the money came from her father. The trip is successful, and Nora works to pay for the loan by herself after the trip. One day, her husband tells her that he is going to fire Krogstad, and Krogstad tells Nora that he will reveal the source of the Italy loan unless she protects his job. Helmer eventually finds out about the loan and becomes extremely upset with his wife, more worried about his image than anything else. He treats his wife like a child even though she saved his life. Nora realizes in that moment that her husband does not respect her as a human being. He does not treat her like an equal, but like a doll, an object whose only job is only to please him. Therefore, Nora decides to leave her husband and her children and discover her real identity, as is illustrated in this scene between Helmer and Nora:

Nora: No, I have never been happy. I thought I was, but it has never really been so.

Helmer: Not—not happy!

Nora: No, only merry. And you have always been so kind to me. But our home has been nothing but a playroom. I have been your doll-wife, just as at home I was papa's doll-child; and here the children have been my dolls. I thought it great fun when you played with me, just as they thought it great fun when I played with them. That is what our marriage has been, Torvald.[3]

Nora's life was restricted to her house, where she entertained her children and her husband. She tries to delight her husband and takes on different characters to amuse him, as illustrated in the following scene with Mrs. Linde, an old friend:

Nora: . . . Tomorrow evening there is to be a fancy-dress ball at the Stenborgs', who live above us; and Torvald wants me to go as a Neapolitan fisher-girl, and dance the Tarantella that I learned at Capri.

Mrs. Linde: I see; you are going to keep up the character.

Nora: Yes, Torvald wants me to. Look, here is the dress; Torvald had it made for me there, but now it is all so torn, and I haven't any idea—[4]

Despite the fact that her husband considers Nora an object, she worked behind her husband's back and has successfully paid for the loan she asked for in order to help him, demonstrating that she is capable of being much more than a doll. When Nora realizes at the end of the play, after Helmer discovers the truth about the loan, that her husband is more worried about his honor than his relationship with her, she says: "I have been performing tricks for you, Torvald. That is how I have survived. You wanted it like that. . . . It's because of you I have made nothing of my life."[5] When Helmer accuses Nora of not fulfilling her duties if she leaves, she tells him that she does not believe that women should be limited to performing those specific duties anymore and rebels against them:

Helmer: It's outrageous. That you can betray your most sacred duties in this way.

Nora: What do you count as your most sacred duties?

Helmer: And I have to tell you! Are they not the duties to your husband and your children?

Nora: I have other equally sacred duties.

Helmer: No, you don't. What "duties" might you have in mind?

Nora: Duties to myself.

Helmer: You are first and foremost a wife and a mother.

Nora: I no longer believe that. I believe that I am first and foremost a human being, just as much as you—or at least, that I will try to become one.[6]

In fact, "When Nora discovers that she has duties higher than those of a 'wife and mother,' obligations she names as 'duties to myself,' she is voicing the most basic of feminist principles: "that women no less than men possess a moral and intellectual nature and have not only a right but a duty to develop it."[7] In his speech to the Norwegian Women's Rights League in 1878, Ibsen indicated that: "A woman cannot be herself in contemporary society, it is an exclusively male society with laws drafted by men, and with counsel and judges who judge feminine conduct from the male point of view."[8] In that same speech, Ibsen voiced his opinion that women deserve freedom and equality, and to gain that, they need to be educated and cannot be given restrictive roles. As Nora explains, she went from being her dad's toy to her husband's toy:

Nora: That's just it. You've never understood me—A great wrong has been done to me, Torvald: First by Papa, and then by you.

Helmer: What! By us two—the two people who have loved you more than anyone else?

Nora: (*Shaking her head*) You never loved me. You just thought it was fun to be in love with me.[9]

At the end of the play, after Helmer scolds her for borrowing the money, Nora asks for a redefinition of what marriage is. She asks to be considered a human being, rather than a woman, because women's restrictive roles do not lead to happiness. In the powerful last scene of the play, Nora slams the door of the house and leaves her husband and children, indicating that she needs to physically leave the oppressive space of the house in order to find out who she really is. Nora's act of leaving the house was immoral because it meant leaving her children and her husband, who were her sacred duties, but she had to do it because it represented society's restrictive roles imposed on women. Women were also supposed to be inside the house to function as moral and religious guides to their children and husbands. Since the public spaces were considered immoral, women could not spend too much time outside their homes without their conduct being questioned: "According to the mores of the time, virtuous women—that is, middle-class, bourgeois

women—were not allowed to venture into the streets without a proper companion. Any woman who was seen on her own in the public spaces of the city
ran the risk of being labeled a public woman, a prostitute."[10] Nora decided to
leave her house, a place that trapped her into roles that she did not find
fulfilling anymore, even though it was considered immoral and despicable
for a woman in the nineteenth century to abandon her husband and children
and venture on her own into the unknown. The house was the only space
available for women in the nineteenth century—a space where they were
forced to raise their children and entertain their husbands. Nora's decision to
leave the house shows her rejection of the nineteenth century ideas of *polis*
and *oikos*, where the public space outside the home was reserved for men.
Men could leave the house to go to work, or to access education or entertainment, but women's space was restricted to the house, that is why Nora
decided to leave and slam the door on her husband's face. In fact, it is the
"women's disproportionate confinement in the private sphere [that] corre-
lates with women's subordinate status."[11] Nora's absence from public spaces
makes her completely dependent on her husband. Helmer controls both the
public and the private spheres because he has the economic power to do so.
Helmer complains to her for having spent too much money on Christmas
gifts and gives her money, warning her that it should last her a while: "Helmer. Don't disturb me. [A little later, he opens the door and looks into the
room, pen in hand.] Bought, did you say? All these things? Has my little
spendthrift been wasting money again?"[12] When Nora suggests borrowing
money, he is condescending to her because she does not make money of her
own and tells her that her idea is stupid and that "That is like a woman!"[13]
When Nora has to secretly work to pay for her debt, she tells Mrs. Linde: "it
was a tremendous pleasure to sit there working and earning money. It was
like being a man."[14] These last two quotes show how a marriage based on
inequality, where the husband has the sole economic control of the household
and dominates the public sphere, is doomed to fail if the woman questions
the set up.

THE HOUSE OF BERNARDA ALBA

Another play that clearly illustrates the metaphor of the house as a place of
moral confinement is Federico García Lorca's *The House of Bernarda Alba*.
García Lorca based his play on the house of a woman called Frasquita Alba,
which was next to his cousin's house in Valderrubio, near Granada. In this
house, the mother Frasquita had exercised a silent tyranny over her daughters
by not allowing them to leave the house very often to preserve their virtue
until her death in 1924. García Lorca writes *The House of Bernarda Alba*

"*para atacar las injusticias sociales, las 'causas que tienen remedio'*" ["to criticize social injustice, 'the causes that had a solution.'"][15]

The House of Bernarda Alba starts with a mourning ritual in Bernarda's house for her second husband's death. Later, we find out that Angustias, the oldest daughter, is the only one who can marry because she inherited a considerable amount of money from Bernarda's first husband. The other four daughters' father however, does not leave them much money, which prevents them from marrying and forces them to be locked up in their house for eight years to mourn their father's death. The youngest sister, Adela, rebels against her mother by wearing a green dress instead of a black one to the wake and later goes crazy, threatening to leave the house in the green dress when she finds out that her sister Angustias is planning to marry her love, Pepe el Romano. Her other sisters, however, convince her to stay in the house and Bernarda's servant, Poncia, tells her that Angustias is weak and will probably die trying to deliver her first child and that she could then become Pepe's wife. After Poncia and Bernarda discuss Angustias's inheritance, Bernarda notices that Adela is wearing makeup, which is forbidden when you are in mourning, and violently cleans her daughter's face. María Josefa, Bernarda's mother, who is always locked up in her room against her will, tells Bernarda that if she prevents her daughters from the freedom they need, that they will be destroyed. Bernarda responds to her mother by locking her up in her room again. Eventually, we find out that Adela never stopped loving Pepe and is having an affair with him, defying her mother and sisters. Adela despairs when she finds out that Martirio, one of her sisters, is also in love with Pepe. She also becomes very upset when she discovers that the town's people stoned a woman who had a baby out of wedlock and murdered the baby, because it reminds her of what could happen to her. Tension escalates among the sisters and Bernarda runs after Pepe with a gun when she finds out that Adela is sleeping with him. Later, Bernarda's daughters hear a gunshot and believe that Pepe is dead, leading Adela to hang herself in her room. Bernarda then tells lies so that the people in the town think that her daughter died a virgin, indicating that she cares more about her family's honor than her daughter's death.

In *The House of Bernarda Alba*, the house is a metaphor for female moral imprisonment. According to Gilbert and Gubar, "The house encompasses the greatest universal significance as a symbol of feminine entrapment."[16] And *The House of Bernarda Alba* is a clear example of how the house is an obstacle for women because it prevents them from having the autonomy and independence they need to have happy lives: "Viewed as a symbol for patriarchal dominance, the house is a closed/off space where the father or paternal figure exercises authority over the other family members."[17] In the case of *The House of Bernarda Alba*, Bernarda, with her belief that women should be confined to the house in order to protect their virtue, represents the patriarchal values imposed on women. She is determined to prevent Adela from leaving the house to meet Pepe in the "corral" even if she has to kill him: "The house is its own little society, a virtual dictatorship in which Bernarda rules. The physical house is the dividing line; it separates inside from outside. . . . Inside the house, the veneer of decency reigns; outside is the corruption. "[18] It is significant that the first stage direction is a description of the physical house: "*Habitación blanquísima del interior de la casa de Bernarda. María JosefaMuros gruesos. Puertas en arco con cortinas de yute rematadas con madroños y volantes.*" ["A very white inner room in Bernarda's house. Thick walls. Arched doorways with jute curtains trimmed with black beads and ruffles."][19] The thick walls remind us of a prison. According to Klein,

> The walls, described as thick, serve Bernarda's purpose of keeping her family's secrets contained within them. They also give rise to some of the metaphorical descriptions of the house, which is referred to alternately as a convent, house of war, and hell itself; it is also a prison for Bernarda's mother and daughters.[20]

The second act leads us to the daughters' rooms, which exposes their secrets to the audience. In other words, a wall has been lifted and the audience can see inside the characters' miserable lives caused by their confinement to the house. By the third act, we are led to the corral, where the lovers have intercourse, indicating Adela's desire to escape from her house, her prison, to experience love:

> Of the play's sixteen female characters, it is Adela that projects most lucidly an awareness of the female body as a means toward self-realization. Of Bernarda's five daughters, it is she who defies most vehemently the spatial confinement imposed upon her. Her desire to break free of her imprisonment and become united with Pepe el Romano is the principal source of dramatic tension in the play. As the play evolves, Adela displays with increasing determination a need to take control of her body in order to express her desire to achieve independence.[21]

André Belamich indicates that Adela "*se convierte en símbolo de rebelión. Y ella habrá triunfado. Morirá pronto, pero después de haber conocido plenamente el amor, y su rival, Martirio, podrá suspirar: 'Dichosa ella mil veces que lo pudo tener'*" ["becomes a symbol of rebellion. And she will have triumphed. She will die soon, but not before she has found out what love is about, and her rival, Martirio, will sigh: 'She is a thousand times lucky because she could have him.'"][22] In his analysis of the play, Morris mentions that the importance of the house as a prison is also symbolized in the repetition of parts of the house, like: "walls," "doors," "windows," throughout the play: "Lorca reinforces what the title merely suggests: that the house is a structure that contains people, restricts their lives, and controls our reactions to them."[23] In addition, the repetition throughout the play of the word "woman" as an entrapped human being emphasizes the idea of womanhood as a curse. Even Magdalena, one of the sisters, comments in the first act: *"Malditas sean las mujeres."* ["Women be damned."][24] She also says: *"Todo menos estar sentada días y días dentro de esta sala oscura."* ["Anything but to be here sitting day after day in this dark room"][25] to what Bernarda answers *"esto tiene ser mujer."* ["That is what it is like to be a woman."][26] In the second act, Adela expresses how she would like to go outside: *¡Ay, quien pudiera salir también a los campos!"* ["Man, how I wish I could go outside to the fields!"][27] Bernarda and her society consider the house a citadel of traditional values and the place where women's sexuality could be controlled:

> *Las convenciones sociales en rigor pervierten las relaciones humanas y transforman lo sexual en pura válvula de escape permitida tan solo para los hombres. . . . La estructura del drama, cuyo eje central es el conflicto entre lo social y lo natural, se proyecta en gran parte mediante una utilización simbólica del espacio.*

> [Social conventions pervert human relations and transform sexuality into an escape valve only for men. . . . The structure of the play, developed around the conflict between the social and the natural, is projected mainly by the use of the space as a symbol.][28]

This idea of the house as a prison is emphasized by the metaphorical language used to describe the different parts of the house. The doors are closed shut, the windows have bars and no one can leave the house, including the grandmother. Even the maid, La Poncia, tells Bernarda: *"Tus hijas viven como metidas en alacena."*[29] ["Your daughters live like they are locked up in a cabinet."] Adela tells her mom that Angustias was spying on the men through "las rendijas del portón" ["the cracks of the gate."][30] When the grandmother, María Josefa, escapes her room to go to the patio, Bernarda says: *"¡Encerradla!"* ["Lock her up!"][31] which reminds us of the concept of the madwoman in the attic. A. Jiménez Lora published a piece titled *"Las que esperan"* ["Those Who Wait"] that describes women as *"cautiMaría Josefavas"* ["captives"] in their houses and "shows women's plight to escape a life in which they feel *"abandonadas, solas, en su espera resignada y muda"* ["abandoned, alone, in their resigned wait and mute."][32] Morris reiterates the idea of the house as a place of confinement by explaining that for Adela, her house is a *"presidio,"* for Angustias, an *"infierno,"* for La Poncia, a *"convent"* ["prison," "hell," "convent,"][33] and for María Josefa a "madhouse."

Both *A Doll's House* and *The House of Bernarda Alba* were written by men who defended the idea of women having the same needs and requiring the same freedom as men. Even though Ibsen never openly admitted being a feminist, he proved in his speech held at the festival of the Norwegian Women's Right League in Christiana that he was concerned with what to him was "a problem of humanity in general."[34] Hassan Balaky agrees that "Ibsen's support of the feminist movement and ideology becomes evident not only through his characters and subject matter of his plays but also through his engagement in the women's cause whether he admitted it or not."[35]

Similar to Ibsen, Lorca was known to show compassion for women's situation in Spain:

> *En su panorámica de la sociedad, Lorca siempre muestra gran compasión por los problemas de las mujeres y sus heroínas, quienes rehusan aceptar la conducta que la sociedad les dicta; si Mariana Pineda, la María JosefaNoviaMaría Josefa, en María JosefaBodas de sangreMaría Josefa y Adela, en María JosefaLa casa de Bernarda AlbaMaría Josefa, se rebelan contra la norma social, Lorca presenta esa rebelión con cierta dosis de comprensión.*

> [In his panoramic view of society, Lorca always shows great compassion for women's problems and his heroines' problems, who refuse to accept the behavior that society imposes on them; if *Mariana Pineda*, la Novia, in *Blood Wedding* and Adela, in *The House of Bernarda Alba*, rebel against the social norms, Lorca portrays this rebellion with a certain dosage of understanding.][36]

We also know that Lorca was influenced by Ibsen and other playrights' preoccupation with women's rights as human rights:

> *Lo que sorprende al estudioso de la obra lorquiana es que Lorca no heredó su actitud compasiva hacia las mujeres del teatro español exclusivamente; también fue influenciado por Ibsen y Chekov.*

> [What surprises the expert on Lorca's work is that Lorca did not inherit his compassionate attitude toward women from Spanish playwrights exclusively; he was also influenced by Ibsen and Chekov.][37]

In sum, women's lives in both *A Doll's House* and *The House of Bernarda Alba* clearly symbolized a life of moral imprisonment while men could do whatever they pleased both inside and outside their homes. The main characters in both plays, must physically leave the house, a place of oppression, in order to be fulfilled.

NOTES

1. A. M. Shanahan, "Playing House: Staging Experiments About Women in Domestic Space," *Theatre Topics*, Vol. 23, No. 2 (2013): 130.

2. Thomas Jefferson, *The Writings of Thomas Jefferson: 1743–1826*, Paul Leicester Ford (ed.), Vol. 10 (1865–1902): 46.

3. Henrik Ibsen, *A Doll's House* (New York: Global Classics, 2014), 63.

4. Ibidem, 30.

5. Ibidem, 63.

6. Ibidem, 64.

7. Joan Templeton, "The Doll House Backlash: Criticism, Feminism, and Ibsen Author(s)," *PMLA*, Vol. 104, No. 1 (January 1989): 29.

8. H. Ibsen, *Speeches and New Letters* (trans. A. Kildal) (Boston: R.G. Badger, Gorham Press, 1910), 65.

9. Henrik Ibsen, *A Doll's House*, ed. cit., 62.

10. Hilde Heinen, "Modernity and Domesticity: Tensions and Contradictions," *Negociating Domesticity*, Hilde Heinen and Gülsüm Baydar (eds.) (London and New York: Routledge, 2005), 10.

11. L. Code (ed.), *Encyclopedia of Feminist Theories* (New York: Routledge, 2000), 342.

12. Henrik Ibsen, *A Doll's House*, ed. cit., 4.

13. Ibidem.

14. Ibidem, 17.

15. All the translations from Spanish to English have been done by me. This sentence was quoted in André Belamich, "El público y *La casa de Bernarda Alba*, polos opuestos en la dramaturgia de Lorca," *La casa de Bernarda Alba y el teatro de García Lorca*, Domenech, Ricardo, ed. (Madrid: Catedra, 1985), 91.

16. Sandra Gilbert and Susan Gubar, *The Madwoman in the Attic: The Woman Writer and the Nineteenth Century Literary Imagination* (New Haven: Yale University Pres, 1979), 88–89.

17. John P. Gabriele, "House and Body: Confinement in Lorca's Woman-Conscious Trilogy," *Hispanic Research Journal*, Vol. 1, No. 3 (October 2000): 276.

18. Ibidem.

19. Federico García Lórca, *Obras Completas*, 20th ed. (Madrid: Aguilar, 1977), 853.

20. Dennis A. Klein, *Blood Wedding, Yerma, and the House of Bernarda Alba: Garcia Lorca's Tragic Trilogy* (Boston: Twayne Publishers, 1991), 128.

21. John P. Gabriele, "House and Body: Confinement in Lorca's Woman-Conscious Trilogy," ed. cit., 282.

22. André Belamich, "El público y La casa de Bernarda Alba, polos opuestos en la dramaturgia de Lorca," *La casa de Bernarda Alba y el teatro de García Lorca*, ed. cit., 88.

23. C. Brian Morris, "The 'Austere Abode': Lorca's 'La casa de Bernarda Alba,'" *Society of Spanish & Spanish-American Studies*, Vol. 11, No. 1/2 (1986): 129.

24. Federico García Lórca, *Obras Completas*, ed. cit., 849.

25. Ibidem.

26. Ibidem.

27. Ibidem, 883.

28. John Crispi, "*La casa de Bernarda Alba* dentro de la visión mítica Lorquiana," *La casa de Bernarda Alba y el teatro de García Lorca*, ed. cit., 180.

29. Federico García Lórca, *Obras Completas*, ed. cit., 915.

30. Ibidem, 851.

31. Ibidem, 868.

32. A. Jiménez Lora, "Las que esperan," *La Alhambra*, Vol. 13, No. 303 (1910): 511.

33. C. Brian Morris, "The 'Austere Abode': Lorca's 'La casa de Bernarda Alba,'" ed. cit., 132–133.

34. H. Ibsen, *Speeches and New Letters* (trans. A. Kildal), ed. cit., 65.

35. Hassan Balaky and Saman Salah, "A Feminist Analysis of Henrik Ibsen's *A Doll's House*," *Beytulhikme: An International Journal of Philosophy*, Vol. 6, No. 1 (June 2016): 38.

36. J. Rey, *El Papel de la Mujer en el Teatro de Federico Garcia Lorca*, (1994). Retrieved from https://ro.ecu.edu.au/theses_hons/611, 98.

37. Ibidem.

Chapter Five

The House as a Magical Space

The House of the Spirits *and* Like Water for Chocolate

Latin American authors of the 1960s, known as the boom writers, explained that the reality in their countries was so hyperbolic and surreal that it was not possible to use realism to describe the events occurring there. Only through magical realism could events like "*la masacre bananera*"[1] in Colombia or Juan Manuel de Rosas's dictatorship in Argentina be explained. Authors like Gabriel García Márquez, Juan Rulfo, and Mario Vargas Llosa portrayed their reality through the use of magical realism to inform the rest of the world of the political, social, and economic situation in Latin America. Everyone's eyes around the world were on Latin America in the 1960s due to the following facts: Venezuela and Mexico had started to export their petroleum, the Cuban Revolution had begun, showing the transformation of a democratic country into a communist one, and the book industry was exploding. These historical events increased global attention toward Latin America, which led to an interest in Latin American authors. However, female Latin American authors such as Isabel Allende or Laura Esquivel were not initially as successful as their male counterparts. In fact, Allende's novel *The House of the Spirits* was forbidden in Chile for a period of time because the novel's political criticism of the right wing upset the Chilean male elites.

This chapter will explore how the novels *The House of the Spirits* by Isabel Allende and *Like Water for Chocolate by* Laura Esquivel use of the house as a metaphor to portray how women defy the patriarchal tradition of restricting women to the space of the house. Through magical realism, both authors show how women rebel against the roles that society imposes on them. In Allende's case, Clara, one of her characters, resists the interpretation of the house as a place for male political discussion and male control, and transforms it into her own magical world, a world that her husband cannot enter or comprehend. In Esquivel's case, her main character Tita escapes suppression by transforming the kitchen into a magical place in which she controls everyone's lives by influencing their behavior through her culinary rituals. Both Clara and Tita are able to escape their confinement at home by creating their own magical worlds.

THE HOUSE OF THE SPIRITS

The House of the Spirits was published in 1982 and describes the life of a family, the Trueba- Del Valles. The story begins when Esteban Trueba asks Rosa la Bella to marry him, but she dies because of a terrible mistake. She accidentally drinks a poisoned drink meant for her father. After some time, Esteban makes a fortune and comes back to marry Rosa's little sister, Clara. Clara, who has not said a word since her sister's death because she feels guilty that she predicted it, talks for the first time and agrees to marry Trueba. After the wedding, the couple moves to "Las tres Marías," a hacienda that Esteban purchased and fixed in order to have a place to raise a family. During this time, the readers are able to see the abuse that the upper classes commit against peasants through Esteban's exploitation of the hacienda workers. We also see his brutality and his concept of women as objects when he rapes one of his peasants repeatedly, resulting in her pregnancy with a boy who is never recognized by Esteban. During that time, he also frequents brothels, where he meets Transito, a prostitute who asks him for money but will help him on a future occasion. When Esteban's sister, Ferula, loses her mom, Clara invites her to live with them. When Clara and Ferula become very close, Esteban becomes jealous and uncomfortable. However, they are both so happy with their bond that they ignore Esteban. One day, Esteban finds them together in bed and forbids Ferula from ever stepping foot in his house again. Clara has a daughter named Blanca, who falls in love with a peasant's son, Pedro. When Esteban finds out, Blanca is sent away to a boarding school to prevent Pedro and her from being together. Nevertheless, every summer, Blanca and Pedro find a way to be together, and Blanca eventually becomes pregnant. Clara tries to protect their daughter Blanca from Esteban when he finds out the news, but he beats Clara. Although she never speaks to him again, she eventually forgives him before dying a few years later. Meanwhile, Esteban campaigns for the office of Senator of the Republic, representing the right wing. When the left wins, the military forces take over and kidnap Blanca, who supported the left wing. After Clara begs Esteban to hide Pedro, he does so and helps him leave the country safely. Transito, the prostitute from his past, helps him save his daughter because she now knows people with political power. The story ends with Blanca coming home to her daughter and later meeting Pedro.

Throughout the novel, Clara defies the idea of men's control of their women in a society in which women did not have the power to make their own decisions and could only be either a wife and a mother, or a prostitute. Clara's capability to predict the future and to see the dead empowers her to help others. She also creates a world of her own in which only women can be a part. Esteban notices her abilities and resents his wife. He first noticed the strong connection between his wife and his sister, and later between his wife and his daughter Blanca. In an essay that appears in a book called *Female and Male in Latin America*, Jane Jaquette describes this concept:

> The Latin American woman correctly perceives role differentiation as the key to her power and influence. Even the notions of the "separateness" and "mystery" of women, which are viewed in the North American context as male propaganda chiefly used to discriminate against women, are seen in the Latin American context as images to be enhanced, not destroyed.[2]

Latin American feminists emphasize the differences between the sexes instead of hiding them. Therefore, having spiritual and supernatural qualities becomes an asset rather than a weakness. Clara's eccentric behavior becomes a weapon to defy patriarchal oppression. Ronie-Richele García-Johnson also agrees that the women in *The House of the Spirits* "depend on their spiritual and emotional strength to survive."[3] We can observe this aspect in the novel when Esteban tried to be the master of the house by transforming it into a forum for political discussion, but Clara did not allow that to happen by carrying out her spiritual activities and by expanding the house to do her charity work. She does not allow her husband to restrict her in a specific space in her own house:

> In response to Clara's imagination and the requirements of the moment, the noble, seigniorial architecture began sprouting all sorts of extra little rooms, staircase, turrets, and terraces. Each time a new guest arrived; the bricklayers would arrive and build another addition to the house. The big house on the corner soon came to resemble a labyrinth.[4]

Esteban tries to regain control of his house but loses the battle and has to allow his wife to have a wide assortment of strangers in their house.

Writing is another way in which Clara has control over her life and her identity. At the beginning of the novel, the narrator describes how Clara already had the habit of writing important things and how, when she lost her voice after her sister's death, she continued writing as a way to tell her story. She creates a female literary tradition that empowers future generations by emphasizing the positive aspects of women having the power of spirituality and the supernatural. Sandra Boschetto describes Clara's writing as a key fact in the creation of her identity: "this female figure responds to a concept of the world based on language as the invention of what is possible."[5] Writing is, therefore, a way in which Clara can escape the limitations imposed by her husband and her society.

Another way in which Clara defies Esteban is that when he beats her, she controls the situation by not talking to him or letting him access the space of her room, of her body: "Clara had refused the masculine body access to her feminine world, and she swore not to enter masculine verbal space. Trueba was, more than frustrated, defeated; he could not touch Clara's soul, let alone control it."[6] When Alba, the daughter of Blanca and Pedro, grows up, she admits that the house bears the soul of her grandmother, which exemplifies the power that Clara had over the house: "Alba knew that her grandmother was the soul of the big house on the corner. Everybody else learned it later, when Clara died and the house lost its flowers, its nomadic friends, and its playful spirits and entered into an era of decline."[7]

Clara is not the only member of Esteban's family who fights against his authority. Blanca, Clara's daughter continues with the tradition of defiance and independence started by her mother by disobeying her father and staying with Pedro despite her father's rage. She leaves the space of her elegant house built by her father to sleep with Pedro in the middle of nature. She rebels against the space imposed on her by escaping through the window to meet her lover. The ultimate insult to her father was conceiving a daughter with Pedro. She later defies her father's orders both by bringing Pedro to his house and by going against his political beliefs as well.

Alba, Clara's daughter, did not run away with her lover, Miguel, but instead brought him to the basement of her grandfather's house to have sex with him. These actions violated not only her grandfather's space, but also the rules of what was expected by of a woman in Chile in the 1960s, which was to be married before having sex. In *The Poetics of Space*, Bachelard discusses the significance of the basement, where the family treasures were located. According to him, lovers went to the basement because their love was "underground," a secret, and a "nest"[8] of love, something against society's rules for women.

Women in *The House of the Spirits* fought for their own space, whether transforming the house as their own magical space, such as Clara, by rebelling against it and escaping it, like Blanca, or by making it their own love nest despite society's rules, like Alba. These women were not afraid of a male chauvinistic figure like Esteban, or their society, and fought to create their own space and to find a place for those not as fortunate. In Gabriela Mora's words, Allende's novels "demonstrate the oppression and the dependence in the woman of the oligarchy as well as in the poor peasant woman."[9]

LIKE WATER FOR CHOCOLATE

Tita, the main character of *Like Water for Chocolate*, also transforms a place of reclusion, the house and the kitchen specifically, into a magical space where anything is possible. Tita falls in love with a man named Pedro, but Mamá Elena does not allow Tita to marry him because, according to an obsolete Mexican tradition of the time, the youngest daughter has to remain unmarried for life in order to take care of her mother. Tita is forced not only to remain single, but also to cook for everyone in the house. After forbidding Tita from marrying Pedro, Mamá Elena offers her oldest daughter Rosaura in marriage to Pedro. Pedro agrees to marry Rosaura only to be close to Tita, but Tita is heartbroken by this situation. Mamá Elena sees Tita and Pedro flirting with each other and decides to send Rosaura and Pedro away. That fact, and the death of her nephew, causes Tita to have a mental breakdown. When Doctor John comes to see Tita, he helps her recover her mental stability, falls in love with her, and asks her to marry him. She initially agrees, but then Pedro and her sister Rosaura move back with their new baby girl, the situation changes. Pedro is very jealous of the fact that Tita has agreed to marry John and seduces her. Tita agrees not to marry John, but her mother's ghost torments Tita and tries to prevent her from sleeping with Pedro. Once Rosaura dies, her daughter marries John's son and Tita and Pedro consummate their love but die from the intense sexual experience of finally being able to be together without any obstacles in their way.

Tita's existence, like other women of the time, was tied to the kitchen. However, Tita uses this to her advantage, using her culinary rituals to empower her and to overcome her entrapment in the kitchen because she is able to control others with her dishes. As Spanos asserts, "What Esquivel does in *Like Water for Chocolate* is to reclaim the kitchen as a place or space of artistic and creative power."[10] Whoever eats a dish that Tita has cooked experiences the same feelings Tita had when she was cooking that meal. When Tita is forced to make her sister's wedding cake, she feels desolate and her feelings are transferred into the cake, making all the guests feel how she feels and therefore ruining her sister's wedding to Pedro. In the scene in which Tita cooks the *"Codornices con pétalos de rosa"* ["Quails with rose petals"], she feels an intense sexual desire for Pedro that is transmitted into her dish. After her sister Gertrudis eats the cake, the heat coming out of her body causes the wooden shower to catch on fire because she cannot help but to feel a strong sexual desire like Tita's. Because of the intense sexual desire caused by Tita's dish, Gertrudis ends up running away with Juan, a fighter in a political battle for peasant liberation, after he runs towards her on a horse. As the above scene illustrates, the effects of Tita's cooking lead other women, such as Gertrudis, to obtain their own liberation against their society's rules. Because of Tita's dish, Gertrudis has an open sexual relation with a man without being married, which was unthinkable for a respectable Mexican woman in the early 1900s.

Tita does not only defy society's expectations of women through her cooking, but she also creates a female tradition that recognizes all the women in previous generations who used their cooking as a way to express themselves creatively and to escape repression. Esperanza, Tita's great niece, explains how Tita's recipes will live forever as long as the future generations cook with them:

> That is why I am preparing Christmas Rolls, my favorite dish. My mama prepared them for me every year. My mama! . . . How wonderful the flavor, the aroma of her kitchen, her stories as she prepared the meal, . . . why my tears flow so freely when I prepare them—perhaps I am sensitive to onions as Tita, my great aunt, who will go on living as long as there is someone who cooks her recipes.[11]

For women in that time period in Mexico, their recipes and their cooking was their way to connect with the women of previous generations: "Tita's recipes were originally handed down orally until she carefully compiled them and wrote them, thus creating a cook-book for her female descendants."[12] When Tita dies, she passes her recipe book to her niece, who will then pass it on to future generations of women. It is important to know that this is not an ordinary cookbook but rather a book that teaches women that they have the power to transform society through their cooking by being creative: "Mama Elena, the representative of society, exiles Tita into the ranch's kitchen. The result is totally unexpected. Instead of enduring her imposed seclusion stoically, Tita challenges it by dispelling common stereotypes that portray Mexican women as passive and unimaginative creatures."[13] The fact that Tita's great niece's name is Esperanza, which means hope in Spanish, reflects the author's idea that there is still hope for women to be heard. If they are locked up in their kitchens, then, they have to stick together, and use their cooking powers to transform society, just like Tita does with her dishes.

Tita's connection with her mother's cook, Nacha, grants her the continuation of a sacred tradition, cooking as a ritual that goes back to Mexico's prehispanic past. Every cooking routine that Nacha teaches Tita has mystical powers. At the same time, like García-Johnson explains in her article "The Struggle for Space: Feminism and Freedom in *The House of the Spirits*," Nacha's teachings take a radical turn when Tita changes or adds a new ingredient to Nacha's recipes. This action subverts the social order because Tita changes a traditional recipe that has been passed on through generations. Tita, like her recipes, changes to defy the established order. Tita starts making her own decisions when she starts changing the recipes, and then becomes her own self when she disobeys her mother by leaving her. Tita transforms from a dutiful daughter to a rebel when she decides to leave her mom to live with Dr. John. When her sister Rosaura tells Tita her intentions of not allowing her daughter to marry so she could take care of her when she was old, Tita responds by cursing her sister: "Tita did not submit. Doubts and anxieties sprang from her mind. For one thing, she wanted to know who started this family tradition. It would be nice if she could let that genius know about one little flaw in this perfect plan for taking care of women in their old age."[14] Tita's defiance becomes so powerful that she has the power over life and death. Rosaura dies from eating Tita's food, which made her corpse bloated and smelly: "the disagreeable odor Rosaura's body gave off got worse after her death. For that reason, not many people chose to attend. The ones determined not to miss it were the buzzards . . . a flock of them circled the funeral party until the body had been buried."[15] Similarly, Mama Elena dies because she was so afraid of being poisoned by Tita that she ingested too much ipecac.

Both Clara and Tita's worlds are populated by women who defy society in a creative way. In *The House of the Spirits*, Clara creates her own world within her house, a world that is separated from her husband's. She has the magical powers to help people, to control her space, and to decide. She decides who can be part of that world. Clara has a stronger connection with the women in her house, including her husband's sister, Ferula, than with her husband, who she isolates when he physically hurts her. She also influences the future generations to live happy independent lives, as is shown in Blanca and Alba's decisions to fight not only for women's rights, but for everyone's rights. Another example of her influence on the future is when Alba sells Esteban's furniture behind his back to finance a children's soup kitchen. In Tita's world, the kitchen, instead of functioning as a place of restriction, becomes, with the use of magical realism, a place of liberation. In the kitchen, Tita is able to express her creativity, to control others, and to leave a legacy for future generations of women through her recipes. Furthermore, Tita does not encourage other women to follow the traditional recipes, but to find their own way to make those recipes work for them. In other words, she removes the restrictions on future generations by allowing them to continue using the same ingredients of the past or to add new ingredients of their own. This freedom is an important change that empowers women to choose what ingredients to use. The strong female characters in both books show their societies that men and society should not impose any specific roles on women: women should be able to make their own choices, create their own destinies.

NOTES

1. "The banana massacre" was an event that happened in 1928 in Ciénaga, Colombia, where a group of workers were murdered by the conservative government of Miguel Abadía

Méndez due to the fact that the workers' strikes were costing the government, the United States and Europe severe financial losses. Both Gabriel García Márquez in *Cien Años de Soledad* and Álvaro Cepeda Samudio in *La Casa Grande* depicted a fictional version of this massacre.

2. Jane Jaquette, "Female and Male in Latin America," *Journal of Inter-American Studies and World Affairs*, Vol. 16, No. 1 (February 1974): 20.

3. Ronie-Richele García-Johnson, "The Struggle for Space: Feminism and Freedom in 'The House of the Spirits,'" *Revista Hispánica Moderna*, Vol. 47, No. 1 (1994): 188.

4. Isabel Allende, *The House of the Spirits* (New York: Atria, 2015), 299.

5. Boschetto, Sandra, "Dialéctica metatextual y sexual en *La casa de los espíritus* de Isabel Allende." *HISPANIA* (Journal of the American Association of Teachers of Spanish and Portuguese) 72.3 (September 1989), 526. Translated by me.

6. Ronie-Richele García-Johson, "The Struggle for Space: Feminism and Freedom in *The house of the Spirits*," *Revista Hispánica Moderna*, Vol. 47, No. 1 (June 1994): 189.

7. Isabel Allende, *The House of the Spirits*, ed. cit., 314.

8. Gaston Bachelard, *The Poetics of Space*, Trans. Maria Jolas (Boston: Beacon Press, 1969).

9. Gabriela Mora, "Las novelas de Isabel Allende y el papel de la mujer como ciudadana," *Ideologies and Literature*, Vol. 2 (1987): 53. This is my own translation.

10. Tony Spanos, "The Paradoxical Metaphors of the Kitchen in Laura Esquivel's *Like Water for Chocolate*," *Letras Femeninas*, Vol. 21, No. 1/2 (Primavera-Otoño 1995): 30.

11. Laura Esquivel, *Like Water for Chocolate* (New York: Anchor Books, Doubleday, 1992), 241.

12. Rosa Fernández-Levin, "'The Last Walls Dissolve': Space Versus Architecture in *The Memoirs of a Survivor* and 'The Yellow Wallpaper,'" *Doris Lessing Studies*, Vol. 28, No. 1 (2009): 107.

13. Ibidem, 108.

14. Laura Esquivel, *Like Water for Chocolate*, ed. cit., 9.

15. Ibidem, 227.

Chapter Six

The House as a Metaphor of Social and Racial Integration

Brown Girl, Brownstones *and* A Raisin in the Sun

Brown Girl, Brownstones by Paule Marshall and *A Raisin in the Sun* by Lorraine Hansberry portray Black American families' struggling to become economically and socially successful, represented by the purchase of a home. In both works, a powerful and strong female character tries to make the dream of owning a home a reality. In *A Raisin in the Sun*, that character is Mama: "Hansberry herself gave Mama the designation of matriarch, asserting that Mama is 'The Black matriarch incarnate: The bulwark of the Negro family since slavery; the embodiment of the Negro will to transcendence.'"[1] In *Brown Girl, Brownstones*, the main character Silla "represents the personality and perseverance of many West Indian women whom Marshall knew as a child—examples of self-propelled, assertive women active in controlling their own spheres of meaningful existence."[2] The male characters in both works represent one of the obstacles that the female characters have to overcome to achieve their dreams. In *A Raisin in the Sun*, Mama's son, Walter, loses his money by making the unfortunate decision to trust the wrong business partners and tries to sell his mom's newly purchased house because he feels threatened by the new white neighbors. Mama and his wife Ruth have to convince him to assert his right to live there:

MAMA (*Opening her eyes and looking into WALTER's*)
No. Travis, you stay right here. And you make him understand what you doing, Walter Lee. You teach him good. Like Willy Harris taught you. You show how our five generations done come to. (*WALTER looks from her to the*

boy, who grins at him innocently) Go ahead, son (*She folds her hands and closes her eyes*) Go ahead.[3]

In *Brown Girls, Brownstones*, Silla's husband, Deighton, is an example of an impractical man who was unable to support his family. A minor character in the play says about Deighton:

> I tell you those men from Bridgetown is all the same. They don't know a thing 'bout handling money and property and thing so. They's spree boys. Every last one of them. . . . There ain nothin wrong with wanting piece of ground home but only when you got a sufficient back prop here. I tell you, he's a disgrace.[4]

In contrast to the men, these books' strong female characters try to assimilate to the new culture by fulfilling the American dream of owning a house.

BROWN GIRL, BROWNSTONES

Brown Girl, Brownstones by Paule Marshall was published in 1959. The novel was based on Marshall's life as a young girl and is the story of Selina Boyce's coming of age. Selina is the daughter of Deighton and Silla Boyce, Barbadian immigrants living in the United States in the 1950s. In the first of the novel's four parts, 10-year-old Selina lives in a rented Brooklyn brownstone with her family. Deighton receives a letter that communicates to him that he has inherited land in his native country. His wife tells him to sell it to buy a brownstone, but he wants to keep the land.

In the second part of the novel, Selina witnesses her parents' arguments at home about what to do with the land. Silla decides that she stills wants to buy a home and tells her friends that she is going to sell the inherited land herself. Selina overhears the conversation and becomes fearful of the possible future of her parents' relationship if her mother goes through with selling the land. In the third part of the book, the United States has entered into World War II, Selina is coming into womanhood, and Silla forges some letters in order to convince Deighton's sister to sell the land in Barbados. When Deighton finds out, he spends the proceeds from selling the land on gifts to avenge his wife's action. When the community finds out what Deighton has done, they all turn their backs on him. Deighton injures his arm at work and cannot work anymore. He then joins a cult that makes him abandon his family to work in a restaurant. Deighton flees to Barbados after Silla calls immigration on him, but he jumps from the boat to his death during the trip back to the island. Selina is very disappointed with her mother about her father's death. In the final part of the book, Selina attends college. She is still angry with her mom and her community, but Miss Thompson, her mentor, convinces her to go to a meeting of the Barbadian Homeowner's and Business Association to learn

more about the community. Selina insults the club members and also begins
a sexual relationship with Clive Springer, an artist who is the son of one of
the members. Selina starts to date Clive, joins a modern dance club, and
eventually joins the Barbadian Association in order to win a scholarship and
use the money to run away with Clive.

Although Selina and Clive perform beautifully in their dance club recital,
she runs into a racist white woman who humiliates her and forces her to
confront her lack of integrity in planning to steal the scholarship money.
After the experience at the dance recital, Selina decides to accept the scholarship, tells her mother the truth about her plans, and leaves Brooklyn to go to
the Caribbean, where she plans to become a performer on a cruise ship.

In *Brown Girl, Brownstones*, owning a house symbolizes Caribbean
American economic and social success. Postcolonial theorists such as Ed-
ward Said and Homi K. Bhabha have expanded the concept of home and its
significance for the exiled. Bhabha's idea of the "unhomely" is relevant and
applicable to African/Caribbean American literature. He defines what the
concept of home means by its absence:

> To be unhomed is not to be homeless, nor can the "unhomely" be easily
> accommodated in that familiar division of social life into private and public
> spheres. The unhomely moment creeps up on you stealthily as your own
> shadow and suddenly you find yourself with Henry James'[s] Isabel Archer, in
> *The Portrait of a Lady*, taking the measure of your dwelling in a state of
> "incredulous terror." . . . The recesses of the domestic space become sites for
> history's most intricate invasions. In that displacement, the borders between
> home and world become confused; and, uncannily, the private and public
> become part of each other, forcing upon us a vision that is as divided as it is
> disorienting.[5]

Since the 1930s, Caribbean Americans have tried to overcome their psychological and cultural displacement by saving their money, purchasing property, and thereby becoming part of the American dream of success:

> Always mindful of the poor economic conditions of their homelands, the West
> Indians believed that with persistent determination and close management of
> even a limited income, anyone could eventually "buy house." The Barbadians,
> especially, who had never owned anything perhaps but for a few poor acres in
> a poor land, loved the houses with the same fierce idolatry as they had the land
> on their obscure islands.[6]

Black Caribbean American females have to fight additional odds to
achieve their dream in a capitalist, white male dominated world. The main
character of *Brown Girl, Brownstones*, Selina, goes on a journey of self-
discovery throughout the novel, a journey in which she has to find a
balance between her new life in America and her cultural heritage from

the West Indies. Throughout the novel, Selina observes how her parents and community strive to belong to their new country, represented by the struggle to own a house: "The house is the central point from which all of the ten-year-old Selina's attempts at self-discovery radiate."[7] At the beginning of the novel, the brownstones are described as an army of superhuman proportions:

> In the somnolent July afternoon, the unbroken line of brownstone houses down the long Brooklyn street resembled an army massed at attention. . . . Behind those grim facades, in those high rooms, life soared and ebbed. Bodies crouched in the position of love at night, children burst from the womb's thick shell, and death, when it was time, shuffled through the halls. First, there had been Dutch-English and Scotch-Irish who had built the houses. . . . But now, in 1939 the last of them were discretely dying behind those shades or selling the houses and moving away. And as they left, the West Indians slowly edged their way in. Like a dark sea nudging its way onto a white beach and staining the sand, they came. The West Indians, especially the Barbadians who had never owned anything perhaps but a few poor acres in a poor land, loved the houses with the same fierce idolatry as they had the land on their obscure islands. . . . . Her house was alive to Selina.[8]

When Selina and her sister fight at the beginning of the novel, the brownstones are personified as a protective mother: "the room, like a dark, fragrant mother tried to soothe her. But she would not be comforted."[9] Selina cannot find comfort in her own house because she is struggling to accept her West Indies identity. She feels like an outsider in New York and is also apprehensive about her approaching womanhood because getting married and having children are not her priorities. In fact, she dismisses the thought of having children: "I'n not having any. I'd never let them chop loose my stomach."[10]

Selina's mom, Silla, on the other hand, exemplifies the image of the influential black matriarchal figure found in other texts of African American, African and Caribbean fiction. In a flashback, Silla remembers early life in their poor rural village in Barbados and this memory is why she is fiercely determined to succeed in the United States. She began working in sugar-cane fields at eight years old and selling mangoes to earn a living, but she believed that she could do much better elsewhere and convinced her mother to borrow the money for her passage to America. For Silla, Barbados represents life in poverty with no chances of improving her condition:

> The rum shop and the church join together to keep we pacify and in ignorance. That's Barbados. It's a terrible thing to know that you gon be poor all yuh life, no matter how hard you work. You does stop trying after a time.

People does see you so and call you lazy. But is ain laziness. It just that you does give up. You does kind of die inside. [11]

Like many other immigrant women who moved to New York City, Silla has no intention of returning to her hometown. Once these women arrive at their new destination, they continually search for better jobs and better housing. Immigrants like Silla were not like any other immigrant group who came to the United States because they had a triple challenge: they were black, Caribbean, and women: "Marshall's uniqueness as a contemporary black female artist stems from her ability to write from these three levels of awareness." [12] Like other Caribbean immigrant women, Silla remained in her new home city and took different jobs to achieve the American dream of success: owning a decent house. Silla initially rents a small apartment in Harlem and then leases a four-story brownstone in Brooklyn. She regularly voices her determination to be financially secure and her ambition for a better life: "Lord lemme do better than this. Lemme rise." [13] Silla's dream is not to lease but own a brownstone. Among West Indians, the ownership of a beautiful home meant overcoming the hurdles of migration. Indeed, nearly every conversation that Silla starts ends with the concept of owning a brownstone, and in order to achieve this, she engages in an endless cycle of labor outside her home. Initially, Silla works five days a week as a maid and then takes the night shift at a plant that produces war supplies. She also earns money at home by preparing famous Barbadian delicacies and selling them on Saturdays in West Indian communities. Even though she has to work long hours for small profits, she enjoys her side business because it provides her with economic independence and control over her own life. In the world of cottage enterprises, Silla competes against men and is successful.

The other women in Silla's community play a vital role in the novel. They have the same dream of owning a house, and they function as moral support for Silla. Her group of friends give her validation and comfort as they gather in her kitchen, the brownstone room where Silla exhibits the most strength and power. Marshall "draws on the elements of female strength, independence, and ability to promote self-worth through communal empowerment." [14] These female immigrants had to not only work long hours to achieve their dream but also deal with racism. When they went to scrub floors, white children would laugh at their blackness and shout "nigger," but the Barbadian women did not react to the harsh words because their only thought was of the "few raw-mout' pennies" at the end of the day which would eventually "buy house." [15]

To achieve their dreams of purchasing a home, Silla believed that women should control their reproductive lives. Her perspective on this topic can be observed in the passage where she gives her friend Virgie Farum a reprimand because she already has several children and is pregnant again: "Woman, you might go hide yourself. These ain ancient days. This ain home that you got to be always breeding like a sow. Got to some doctor and get something 'cause these Bajan men will wear you out making children and the blasted children ain nothing but a keep back. You don see the white people having no lot."[16] In America, immigrant women could not afford to have many children as they did in the West Indies because that would deter them from achieving the American dream of owning a house.

Silla knows what she wants and is determined to achieve it, even if it means not having many children and having several jobs. However, her strength is often interpreted as emasculating her husband: "the strength of black women has been too often misinterpreted as an emasculating power."[17] The fact that Silla is the primary provider in her family causes her husband, Deighton, to feel less important, and he decides to have an affair as a way to try to regain his manhood. Because of Silla's independence and community support, she is able to overlook his affair. The breaking point between Silla and Deighton comes when he receives a letter from Barbados informing him that he has inherited several acres of land from his sister, and he does not agree with his wife on what to do with the money. As mentioned before, Silla would like him to sell the land so they can buy their own home in Brooklyn. However, Deighton sees this as an opportunity to return to Barbados as a successful man. Although Silla does not have the opportunity to achieve her dream of owning a house at the end of the novel, she sets the example of female strength and determination for her daughter, as is shown in the fact that Selina decides to go to Barbados "to be her own woman."[18] As she is leaving her neighborhood, she is thinking of what she wants for her future: "Peace, perhaps, as fleeting as that was, and the things that shaped it: love, a clearer vision, a place."[19] This last word indicates that her mother's dream and other black American women's dream of owning a home is now Selina's dream as well, and she is determined to find the strength to fight to achieve that dream.

A RAISIN IN THE SUN

A Raisin in the Sun is a play written by Lorraine Hansberry that debuted on Broadway in 1959. It tells the story of an African American family, Walter and Ruth Younger, their son Travis, Walter's mother (Mama), and Walter's sister Beneatha, who lives in poverty in a dilapidated apartment in Chicago. Walter works as a limousine driver, but he is not happy with the amount of money he makes and wants to be wealthy. To do that, he would like to invest in a liquor store with his friends Willy and Bobo. When Mama's husband dies and she receives a life insurance check for $10,000, Walter would like to use the money to open the liquor store, but Mama has religious objections to alcohol. Eventually, Mama decides to use some of the life insurance money on a down payment on a new house, choosing an all-white neighborhood over a black one because it is cheaper. She decides to give the rest of the money to Walter to invest but tells him to save $3,000 for Beneatha's education. Walter gives all of the money to Willy, who then runs away with it and leaves Walter and Beneatha with nothing. At the same time, Karl Lindner, a white representative of the neighborhood they plan to move to, tries to buy them out to avoid neighborhood tensions over blacks moving into in an all-white neighborhood. Walter wants to accept the offer as a solution to their financial setback.

As the story unfolds, we can observe the contrast between the two men in Beneatha's world, George Murchison, her rich, educated boyfriend, a "fully assimilated black man" that denies his African heritage, and Joseph Asagai, who accepts his African heritage but is poor and uneducated. Joseph criticizes her for assimilating herself into white ways by straightening her hair and for her materialism when she loses the inheritance money. She accepts the fact that she would have to overwork to earn money and accepts Joseph's marriage offer and his idea of moving to Africa with him because she is starting to appreciate her African identity . On the other hand, Walter decides that the only way to obtain wealth is by assimilating to George's culture, which means denying his African roots. In the final scene of the play, Walter later changes his mind and does not accept the buyout offer, stating that they are proud of who they are and deciding to move to their new house in the white neighborhood.

In Chicago in the 1920s, housing segregation increased dramatically for African Americans, and wealthy black Americans tried to buy houses in white neighborhoods in order to escape from a life in the so-called ghetto. Nevertheless, after moving in, they often found themselves targets of violence and racism. To enforce racial boundaries, the Chicago Real Estate Board enacted restrictive covenants that segregated Chicago's black neighborhoods by the end of the decade. As a result of such policies, not enough housing was available for the black population in the 1930s, and they had to pay a more significant percentage of money for their homes than the white population. We can observe this historical aspect in the play *A Raisin in the Sun*, when Mama explains that she had to buy a house in a white neighborhood because "Them houses they put up for colored in them areas way out all seem to cost twice as much as other houses."[20] Hansberry's father was the head of a major real estate corporation, Hansberry Enterprises, and he became affluent during the Depression. In the 1940s, affluent black Americans were not able to find housing that reflected their economic success. In fact, Hansberry's family lived in four different apartments from 1930 to 1938 because of the lack of housing. So in 1938, Hansberry's father began a campaign to defy legal segregation when he decided to buy a house in a white neighborhood, which he was only able to do because of the depressed white housing market. Only three black families lived in that area, and they were constantly harassed. Lorraine Hansberry attended a school where she was one of the few black children, and she remembers "being spat at, cursed and pummeled in the daily trek to and from school."[21] Hansberry also remembers her mom "patrolling [her] house all night with a loaded German luger, doggedly guarding her four children."[22] Hansberry acknowledges the central role that her mother played in her life. According to her, she was a woman whose courage carried them through their struggle to fight racism and to have a relatively normal life in a safe home, while "Daddy spent most of his time in Washington fighting his case."[23] In *A Raisin in the Sun*, Mama's character is likely based on Hansberry's mother. She is the character who proposes the move toward desegregated housing; she fights for her rights to own a decent home: "It is a plain little old house—but it's made good and solid—and it will be ours."[24] Ruth, Mama's daughter-in-law, influenced by her, shows the same strength and enthusiasm to own a house that Mama has at the end of the play: "I'll work . . . I'll work twenty hours a day in all the kitchens in Chicago . . . I'll strap my baby on my back if I have to and scrub all the floors in America and wash all the sheets in America if I have to—but we got to MOVE! We got to get OUT OF HERE!"[25] The events in the play are similar to a housing struggle that unfolded in Wilmington, Delaware, in April 1959 and was reflected in the *Pittsburgh Courier*. In both cases, "it is the Negro women who have the stiffest backbone when it comes to standing with one's back against the wall and slugging it out in the field of civil rights."[26] In *The Raisin in the Sun*, Mama is described as tall and dignified: "Her bearing is perhaps most like the noble bearing of the women of the Hereros of Southwest Africa."[27] Embodying the tradition of African American mothers, she is "the black matriarch incarnate; the bulwark of the Negro family since slavery; the embodiment of the Negro will to transcendence."[28] She works as a cleaning lady and does whatever she has to do to survive and support her family:

> It is she who, while seeming to cling to traditional restraints, drives the young on into the fire hoses and one day simply refuses to move to the back of the bus in Montgomery, or goes out and buys a house in an all-white community where her fourth child and second daughter will almost be killed by a brick thrown through the window by a shrieking racist mob.[29]

Hansberry acknowledges that it is both simultaneously tyrannical and heroic; however, she believed that "the development of strong black women was a gain for the entire race."[30]

Inspired by Du Bois, Robeson, and Hughes, Hansberry insisted that Black families are American families with reasonable aspirations for decent housing and social respect: "In 1959, 'American values' were commonly defined as upward mobility, consumer acquisition, and family privacy."[31] This upward mobility consisted of owning a house in an affordable and safe neighborhood, even if that meant moving to a white neighborhood and having to fight racism in Chicago in the 1960s. Several critics agree that the play represents the "struggle against the mounting odds of a society manifested by slum dwellings, restricted covenants, and a no-exit kind of life."[32] A *Defender* newspaper reviewer also emphasized that Hansberry's main topic was "Chicago's restrictive covenant and other housing problems."[33] Hansberry herself has stated: "Our people don't really have a choice. We must come out of the ghettos of America because the ghettos are killing us."[34]

Brown Girl, Brownstones and *A Raisin in the Sun* depict strong Black female characters that must defy society's racism, and even the men in their family, to provide a better life for their children. Owning a house symbolized an improvement in social and economic status as well as safety for their loved ones, so they did whatever was necessary to work toward that goal.

NOTES

1. Trudier Harrier, *Saints, Sinners and Saviors: Strong Black Women in African American Literature* (New York: Palgrave, 2001), 24.

2. Dorothy Hamer Denniston, *The Fiction of Paule Marshall: Reconstructions of History, Culture and Gender*, ed. cit., 9.

3. Lorraine Hansberry, *A Raisin in the Sun* (New York: Random House, 1951), 147.

4. Paule Marshall, *Brown Girl, Brownstones* (New York: Dover Publications, 1959; 2009), 44.

5. Homi K. Bhabha, *The Location of Culture* (New York: Routledge, 2004), 13.

6. Quoted in Dorothy Hamer Denniston, *The Fiction of Paule Marshall: Reconstructions of History, Culture and Gender* (Knoxville: The University of Tennessee Press, 1983), 10.

7. Patricia Bond-Hutto, "Determined Players in a Fixed Game: A Study of the Black Heroine in Selected Urban Novels by African American Women Writers" (Atlanta: Emory University, Diss., 1993), 205.

8. Paule Marshall, *Brown Girl, Brownstones*, ed. cit., 1–2.

9. Ibidem, 5.

10. Ibidem, 49.

11. Ibidem, 53.

12. Dorothy Hamer Denniston, *The Fiction of Paule Marshall: Reconstructions of History, Culture and Gender*, ed. cit., xiii.

13. Paule Marshall, *Brown Girl, Brownstones*, ed. cit., 214.

14. Dorothy Hamer Denniston, *The Fiction of Paule Marshall: Reconstructions of History, Culture and Gender*, ed. cit., xxi.

15. Paule Marshall, *Brown Girl, Brownstones*, ed. cit., 7.

16. Ibidem, 76.

17. Dorothy Hamer Denniston, *The Fiction of Paule Marshall: Reconstructions of History, Culture and Gender*, ed. cit., xxi.

18. Ibidem, 265.

19. Ibidem.

20. Lorraine Hansberry, *A Raisin in the Sun*, ed. cit., 93.

21. Judith Smith, "Reracializing the Ordinary American Family: *A Raisin in the Sun*," *Visions of Belonging* (New York: Columbia University Press, 2015), 287.

22. Ibidem.

23. Ibidem.

24. Lorraine Hansberry, *A Raisin in the Sun*, ed. cit., 92.

25. Ibidem, 140.

26. Judith Smith, "Reracializing the Ordinary American Family: *A Raisin in the Sun*," ed. cit., 316.

27. Lorraine Hansberry, *A Raisin in the Sun*, ed. cit., 39.

28. Judith Smith, "Reracializing the Ordinary American Family: *A Raisin in the Sun*," ed. cit., 317.

29. Ibidem, 320.

30. Ibidem, 316.

31. Ibidem.

32. Ibidem, 317.

33. Ibidem, 318.

34. Quoted in Judith Smith, "Reracializing the Ordinary American Family: *A Raisin in the Sun*," ed. cit., 321.

Conclusion

The image of the house is very common in world literature. In American novels in particular, the house occupies an important space because the United States is a country whose history has been centered on the business of settlement. Indeed, the American Dream still expresses itself in the hope of owning a house. Both historically and in fiction, possessing a house was traditionally a symbol of economic, social, and even political success. Throughout feminist literary history, the metaphor of the house has constituted a sign of economic freedom and a means to express female identity, but also a symbol of physical or moral entrapment. This dichotomy has been explored by feminist writers whose work often demonstrates how women struggle to have the economic, political, and social power that the white Anglo-Saxon males have always had.

Women's experience is very often linked to the home, especially to the kitchen, while males' space was the study. This clear-cut spatial boundary between men and women within the house indicates a division of roles imposed on them that prevented women from doing intellectual work and relegated them to maternal and household duties. Therefore, many women writers in the nineteenth and twentieth centuries depicted the house as a metaphor of female enslavement and imprisonment and male guardianship, as in Kate Chopin's *The Awakening*, Charlotte Perkins Gilman's "The Yellow Wallpaper," Jean Rhys's *Wide Sargasso Sea*, Henry Ibsen's *A Doll House* and Federico García Lorca's *La casa de Bernarda Alba*.

In the twentieth century, many writers also used the metaphor of the house to define the female self within a larger community. In Edith Wharton's *The House of Mirth*, the house symbolized the patriarchal ideology that oppressed women by denying them any options outside the context of marriage. In works like *Brown Girl, Brownstones* by Paule Marshall and *A*

Raisin in the Sun by Lorraine Hansberry, we can observe how Black American families' symbol of success in the United States, and their way of integrating into their communities, was represented by the ownership of a home.

The emphasis on the house as a metaphor in feminist literature is also present in the 1980s in Latin America. During this time, world readers began to pay more attention to Latin American female writers such as Isabel Allende or Laura Esquivel, who illustrate the significance of houses. In *The House of the Spirits* by Allende and *Like Water for Chocolate* by Esquivel, the authors use magical realism to portray how women defy the patriarchal tradition of restricting women to the space of the house. In *The House on Mango Street* by Sandra Cisneros, readers can see how Chicana women also struggle to have a physical and literary space of their own. However, in order to achieve that goal, they have to fight against a male dominated culture, racism, and sometimes the idea of living in between, or in Gloria Anzaldua's words, "on the border"[1] of two cultures, two races and two languages as well.

Through the study of the metaphor of the house in the works examined here, we see that women in different countries were given roles that were restrictive and often led to unhappiness, such as the roles of housewives and mothers. Their lives were confined to the house, where they were supposed to fulfill those roles in a very particular, constricting way. These restrictive roles are why many characters are seen leaving the house and even committing suicide; it seems these women were unwilling or unable to fulfill society's expectations of them and had not other options. Confined to the house and unable to support themselves, many women had no way of freeing themselves from abuse. For other women, however, the house had a positive connotation, as it represented the American dream of success, a safe place of their own where they could feel like they could fully belong to American society. The house also represented a place where women could write and continue with the female literary tradition as is portrayed in Virginia Woolf's essays and Sandra Cisneros's novels. While the house as a symbol can have many connotations—positive, negative, and intertwined—it is undeniable that it plays an essential role in feminist literature.

NOTE

1. Gloria Andalzúa, *La Frontera: The New Mestiza* (San Francisco, CA: Spinters, 1987).

Bibliography

Allende, Isabel. *The House of the Spirits*. New York: Atria, 2015.

Andalzúa, Gloria. *La Frontera: The New Mestiza*. San Francisco, CA: Spinters, 1987.

Bachelard, Gaston. *The Poetics of Space: The Classic Look at How We Experience Intimate Places*. Boston: Beacon Press, 1994.

Belamich, André. "El público y La casa de Bernarda Alba, polos opuestos en la dramaturgia de Lorca." *La casa de Bernarda Alba y el teatro de García Lorca*, Domenech, Ricardo, ed., Madrid: Catedra, 1985.

Bhabha, Homi K. *The Location of Culture*. 1994. New York: Routledge, 2004.

Bond-Hutto, Patricia. "Determined Players in a Fixed Game: A Study of the Black Heroine in Selected Urban Novels by African American Women Writers." Atlanta: Emory University, Diss., 1993.

Boschetto, Sandra. "Dialéctica metatextual y sexual en *La casa de los espíritus* de Isabel Allende." *HISPANIA* (*Journal of the American Association of Teachers of Spanish and Portuguese*), Vol. 72, No. 3 (September 1989).

Cisneros, Sandra. *A House of My Own: Stories from My Life*. New York: Vintage Books, 2016.

————. *The House on Mango Street*. New York: Vintage Books, 2009.

Code, L. (ed). *Encyclopedia of Feminist Theories*. New York: Routledge, 2000.

Davidson, Carol Margaret. "Haunted House/Haunted Heroine: Female Gothic Closets in *The Yellow Wallpaper*." *Women Studies*, Vol. 33, No. 1 (2004): 47–75.

Denniston, Dorothy Hamer. *The Fiction of Paule Marshall: Reconstructions of History, Culture and Gender*. Knoxville: The University of Tennessee Press, 1983.

Ellis, Kate. "Can you Forgive Her? The Gothic Heroine and Her Critics." *A Companion to the Gothic*. Ed. David Punter. Oxford: Blackwell, 2000.

Ellis, Kate Ferguson. *The Contested Castle: Gothic Novels and the Subversion of Domestic Ideology*. University of Illinois Press, 1989.

Esquivel, Laura. *Like Water for Chocolate*. New York: Anchor Books, Doubleday, 1992.

Farguharson, Kathy. "'The Last Walls Dissolve': Space Versus Architecture in *The Memoirs of a Survivor* and 'The Yellow Wallpaper.'" *Doris Lessing Studies*, Vol. 28, No. 1 (2009).

Fernández-Levin, Rosa. "Ritual and 'Sacred Space' in Laura Esquivel's *Like Water for Chocolate*." *Confluencia*, Vol. 12, No. 1 (Fall 1996).

Gabriele, John P. "House and Body: Confinement in Lorca's Woman-Conscious Trilogy." *Hispanic Research Journal*, Vol. 1, No. 3 (October 2000).

García Lórca, Federico. *Obras Completas*. 20th ed. Madrid: Aguilar, 1977.

————. *Three Plays: Blood Wedding, Yerma, The House of Bernarda Alba*. Trans. Michael Dewell and Carmen Zapata. New York: Farrar, Straus and Giroux, 1993.

García-Johnson, Ronie-Richele. "The Struggle for Space: Feminism and Freedom in *The house of the Spirits.*" *Revista Hispánica Moderna*, Año 47, No 1 (Jun. 1994).

Gilbert, Sandra M., and Susan Gubar. *The Madwoman in the Attic: The Woman Writer and the Nineteenth-Century Literary Imagination*. New Haven and London: Yale University Press, 2020 (1984).

Gilman, Charlotte Perkins. "The Yellow Wallpaper." Sweden: Wisehouse Classics, 2016.

Hansberry, Lorraine. *A Raisin in the Sun*. New York: Random House, 1951.

Harrier, Trudier. *Saints, Sinners and Saviors: Strong Black Women in African American Literature*. New York: Palgrave, 2001.

Hassan Balaky, Saman Salah. "A Feminist Analysis of Henrik Ibsen's *A Doll's House.*" *Beytulhikme An International Journal of Philosophy*, Vol. 6, No. 1 (June 2016).

———. *Speeches and New Letters* (trans. A. Kildal), Boston: R.G. Badger, Gorham Press, 1910.

Heinen, Hilde. "Modernity and Domesticity: Tensions and Contradictions." *Negociating Domesticity*, Hilde Heinen and Gülsüm Baydar (eds.). London and New York: Routledge, 2005.

Ibsen, Henrik. *A Doll's House*. New York: Global Classics, 2014.

Jaquette, Jane. "Female and Male in Latin America." *Journal of Inter-American Studies and World Affairs*, Vol. 16, No. 1 (February 1974).

Jefferson, Thomas. *The Writings of Thomas Jefferson: 1743–1826*, Paul Leicester Ford (ed.), Vol. 10 (1865–1902), 46.

Johnson, Erica L. *Home, Maison, Casa: The Politics of Location in Works by Jean Rhys, Marguerite Duras, and Erminia Dell'Oro*. Cranbury, NJ: Rosemont Publishing and Printing, 2003.

Judge, J. "On Their Own: Women Taking Control of Their Lives." *Changing English: Studies in Reading & Culture*, Vol. 10, No. 2 (2003).

Kahane, Claire. "The Gothic Mirror." *The Mother Tongue: Essays in Feminist Psychoanalytic Interpretation*. Eds. Shirley Nelson Garner, Claire Kahane, and Madelon Sprengnether. Ithaca and London: Cornell University Press, 1985.

Kaplan, Amy. *The Social Construction of Realism*. Chicago: University of Chicago Press, 1988.

Killeen, J. "Mother and Child: Realism, Maternity, and Catholicism in Kate Chopin's *The Awakening.*" *Religion & the Arts*, Vol. 7, No. 4 (2003).

Klein, Dennis A. *Blood Wedding, Yerma, and the House of Bernarda Alba: Garcia Lorca's Tragic Trilogy*. Boston: Twayne Publishers, 1991.

Kuhl, Sarah. "*The Angel in the House* and Fallen Women: Assigning Women their Places in Victorian Society." open.conted.ox.ac.uk, *Open Educational Resources* (July 11, 2016): 171–178. https://open.conted.ox.ac.uk/resources/documents/angel-house-and-fallen-women-assigning-women-their-places-victorian-society.

Kress, Jill M. *The Figure of Consciousness: William James, Henry James, and Edith Wharton*. New York and London: Routledge, 2002.

Lydon, Susan. "Abandoning and Re-inhabiting Domestic Space in Jane Eyre, Villette and Wide Sargasso Sea." *Bronte Studies*, 35, 1.

Marshall, Paule. *Brown Girl, Brownstones*. New York: Dover Publications (1959) 2009.

McGee, Diane E. *Writing the Meal: Dinner in the Fiction of Twentieth-Century Women Writers.* Toronto: University of Toronto Press, 2002.

Minh-ha, Trinh H. "Wanderers Across Language." *Elsewhere, Within Here: Immigration, Refugees and the Boundary Event*. London: Routledge, 2011.

Mora, Gabriela. "Las novelas de Isabel Allende y el papel de la mujer como ciudadana." *Ideologies and Literature*, 2 (1987).

Morris, C. Brian. "The 'Austere Abode': Lorca's 'La casa de Bernarda Alba.'" *Society of Spanish & Spanish-American Studies*, Vol. 11, No. 1/2 (1986): 129.

Petty, Leslie. "The Dual-ing Images of la Malinche and la Virgen de Guadalupe in Cisneros's *The House on Mango Street*" (Critical Essay). *MELUS*, Vol. 25, No. 2 (Summer 2000).

Philp, Alexandra. "The Geography of Jean Rhys: The Impact of National Identity upon the Exiled Female Author." *Transnational Literature*, Vol. 9, No. 1 (November 2016).

Quirk, Tom, and Gary Scharnhorst,. "Feminism." *American History Through Literature: 1870–1920, Thomson and Gale*, Vol. 1 (2006).

Ramos, Peter. "Unbearable Realism: Freedom, Ethics and Identity in *The Awakening.*" *College Literature* Vol. 37, No. 4 (2010).

Rey, J. (1994). *El Papel de la Mujer en el Teatro de Federico Garcia Lorca.* Retrieved from https://ro.ecu.edu.au/theses_hons/611.

Rooks, Amanda Kane. "Reconceiving the Terrible Mother: Female Sexuality and Maternal Archetypes in Kate Chopin's *The Awakening.*" *Women's Studies*, Vol. 45 (2016).

Rhys, Jean. *Wide Sargasso Sea.* London and New York: Norton, 2016.

Scanlan, Sean. "Going no Place?: Foreground Nostalgia and Psychological Spaces in Wharton's *The House of Mirth.*" *Style*, Vol. 44, Nos. 1 and 2 (Spring/Summer, 2010).

Shanahan, AM. "Playing House: Staging Experiments About Women in Domestic Space." *Theatre Topics*, Vol. 23, No. 2 (2013).

Spanos, Tony. "The Paradoxical Metaphors of the Kitchen in Laura Esquivel's *Like Water for Chocolate.*" *Letras Femeninas*, Vol. 21, No. 1/2 (Primavera-Otoño 1995).

Smith, Judith. "Reracializing the Ordinary American Family: *A Raisin in the Sun,*" *Visions of Belonging.* New York: Columbia University Press, 2015.

Solomon, Julie Robin. "Staking Ground: The Politics of Space in Virginia Woolf's *A Room of One's Own* and *Three Guineas.*" *Women Studies*, Vol. 16 (1989).

Templeton, Joan. "The Doll House Backlash: Criticism, Feminism, and Ibsen Author(s)." *PMLA*, Vol. 104, No. 1 (January 1989): 29.

Veblen, Thorstein. *The Theory of the Leisure Class.* New York: Penguin Books, 1967.

Von Rosk, Nancy. "Spectacular Homes and Pastoral Theaters: Gender, Urbanity and Domesticity in The House of Mirth." *Studies in the Novel*, Vol. 33, No. 3 (Fall 2001), The John Hopkins University Press.

Wharton, Edith; Ogden Codman Jr (ed.). *The Decoration of Houses.* London: B.T. Batsford, 1898.

———. *The House of Mirth.* South Carolina: Columbia, 2020.

Woolf, Virginia. *A Room of One's Own.* Mariner, 1989.

Index

About the Author

Dr. **Maria Davís** is a scholar in Latin American and American literature, with focus on the Latin American boom writers and twentieth-century American theater, respectively. She also has a master's degree in Teaching Spanish as a Foreign Language. She has published many articles and four books on American Literature, Latin American Literature, Spanish Conversation, and Spanish Culture. She currently teaches at Oxford College of Emory. She just published a book on Short Film for Spanish Conversation called *Vámonos al cine*. She is currently working on a new book on Spanish for beginners called *Hola, ¿qué tal?: A Communicative Approach to Learning Spanish.*

Printed in Great Britain
by Amazon

34296521R00051